What others are saying

"*Abba's Daughter* is filled with the Word of God and will inspire women, young and old, to understand who they are based on the principles God blessed us with. It is a book I will recommend to women I come in contact with. Jennifer's honesty and boldness to share Truth from the Word will strengthen you in your walk, and spur you on in the race called life. May these Truths bring LIFE to your soul. May the words in this book renew your spirit and make you realize that YOU are LOVED by your Creator - Someone you can call Abba."

-Rose Horton, pastor, author, and co-founder of Touched by Grace Ministries

"I found this book easy to read and engaging, with a profound message to women in all walks of the Christian life. It challenges us to listen to God's truth about who we are in Him versus the lies the world tries to make us believe. I highly recommend *Abba's Daughter* as inspiration to find our identity in the Father who chooses us, loves us, and gives us new birth, forgiveness and inner beauty, as He showers us with grace."

-Kirsten Nelson- missionary to Honduras with Legacy Mission International

"I struggle to find the words to explain what reading *Abba's Daughter* has done for my heart. Each chapter took me deeper into the Father's love. Nothing is more life changing then knowing you are a child of the Father, wholly accepted and dearly loved! This is a book that should be read... and re-read, every time we need a reminder!"

-Delores Sleadd, clinical associate at Place of Hope and president of Columbia Aglow Community Lighthouse, Columbia, TN

"By guiding us to wrestle deeply with who we are in Christ, Jennifer Bennett paves for us a path of practical truths baked in biblical theology. *Abba's Daughter* will benefit new believers and those like me, who have been a Jesus follower for a very long time. Although I know who God is, it was refreshing to be reminded of how God sees me and how important is it to see myself as God does. A powerful quick read with practical application to change your life."

"Abba's Daughter" offers a Biblical perspective to help women of all ages find their true identity and worth in Christ. As a mother of two young daughters, I cannot think of anything more important in our present culture than arming them with the Biblical truths that are discussed in this book."

"Jennifer will inspire you as she shares her story of struggle in growing to know God as her Abba Father. As she guides the reader to the heart of God and His Word, Jennifer gently shares the truths she has gleaned over years of walking with The Lord. *Abba's Daughter* was an easy read and filled with encouragement for your soul. Jennifer has a desire to see women walking in the confidence and security of knowing whose they are and how much they are loved by Jesus Christ. Whether you are a seeker, new believer, or seasoned follower of Christ, this book will speak to your heart."

Abba's Daughter:

Embracing Your Identity as a Child of God

Jennifer Bennett

To my children. I wrote this book with you on my heart.
I pray you will know and believe in all that God created you
to be and that you will live in the fullness of that truth.

"See what kind of love the Father has given to us,

that we should be called children of God;

and so we are."

1 John 3:1

Table of contents

Acknowledgements

Bill, Kellie, and Russell: thank you for supporting me, challenging me, and cheering me on. You guys give me reason every day to seek the heart of our Heavenly Father so that, by His strength, I can be the wife, mother, and heavenly daughter He has called me to be. I love you bunches and manys!

Kathy, Lynn, and Delores: your faithful prayers throughout this entire process have sustained and encouraged me. Without you, this dream may have never made the leap into reality. Saying thank you does not express the depth of gratitude I have for you, my sisters in Christ.

Heavenly Father: thank You for lifting me out of the pit I was in and inviting me on this journey with You. May the truths You've taught me be manifest in all I do, that my life would be a true reflection of Your love and grace.

Introduction

"For this reason I bow my knees before the Father,

from whom every family

in heaven and on earth is named."

Ephesians 3:14-15

I remember vividly the day God put the idea for this book on my heart. Although I'm not very good at recalling dates and times—things most people might find important—I do seem to hang on to less significant details. For instance, I remember exactly where I was, what I was doing, and even what I was wearing that day. It was sometime in 2011. I was home alone (an unusual occurrence at our house), and I was wearing a loose-fitting gray shirt with a collar that draped around my neck. I also had on my favorite dark-blue skinny jeans and tall black boots.

The natural light in our living room was growing dim as the afternoon sun cast shade over the back of our house. As I sat curled up on the couch, hugged by cushions that had grown soft from the years of children playing, jumping, and climbing all over them, I found myself in a rare time of quiet. And although the tranquil hour held the promise of refreshment, my heart was heavy. My thoughts were full of concern for my sweet daughter. She was fifteen at the time, and she'd hit those difficult years most of us girls experience. And she was *really* struggling.

She was struggling with her identity. Struggling with her self-worth. Struggling to find her place and purpose. My beautiful girl was struggling between embracing who God had created her to be and who the

4

world was telling her she should be. And, on that particular day, it looked as if the world was winning.

I knew how she was feeling, and I was familiar with the battle she was fighting because I had walked in her shoes. In fact, I felt like I'd worn the tread right off their soles. Not until I was well into my twenties had I begun to discover what would eventually free me from that struggle—understanding the reality of God as my Father and learning to appreciate my identity as His daughter.

Most church-attenders have heard God referenced as Heavenly Father; in fact, Jesus taught His disciples to address God that way in prayer (see Matthew 6:9-13). For many of us, though, this is not a well-developed aspect of the Christian faith. The concept of God being our Abba, *Abba* being an endearing Aramaic word for father that expresses trust and affection, is a vague concept we sort of know about but never really apply to our lives as a foundational reality. The exciting truth is that getting to know God as our perfect Parent and recognizing who we are because we are His children can radically change our lives.

I should note, though, that trusting God as a good Father can be difficult initially—especially for those whose earthly fathers were less than trustworthy. That's because fathers tend to shape a child's first impressions of what the Heavenly Father is like. Though many have wonderful fathers who fill their lives with love and laughter in the formative years, others have fathers who are distant or even cruel. And for better or worse, we tend to apply those earthly examples to the mental pictures we paint of our Father in Heaven.

My own story may help to illustrate this principle. I was the youngest of three: my brother was the hero child, always strong and brave, and my sister was the overachiever who got good grades and never got into trouble. I, by contrast, was curious (read "mischievous"), busy, and very out-of-the-box in my approach to most things I did. The bar in our family was set very high, especially in the world of academics, and for this unscholarly girl who struggled in school, that bar seemed hopelessly out of reach. That's why I began to look for lower, more attainable bars that seemed like they'd be much more fun to attain.

I think that because I didn't fit the neat and tidy mold the rest of my family seemed to fall into easily, my dad was unsure what to do with me. And while I adore him today and am thankful for the relationship we have, I never really felt loved by him in my childhood. I never felt like I was good enough for him. He worked a lot and wasn't very affectionate. And while I do have some special memories of times we shared when I was a child, they seem few and far between. I know now that he loved me as much as he could, in the best way he knew, but to my little-girl heart his actions didn't translate well. I grew up believing that I would never measure up to or be worthy of his love or approval. And for a time, I assumed the same things about God.

Maybe you've long enjoyed a great relationship with your earthly father and can't relate to that feeling I describe. Yet you still find yourself skeptical that God is the perfect Parent that Scripture claims He is, even if you've been a Christian for years. Maybe you look around at the world with all its pain and suffering and wonder how a loving God could allow such evil. If so, know that in our humanity, we tend to place the blame on a God we perceive to be aloof and withdrawn when in fact it's human sin—mankind's general rebellion against God—that's causing all the world's problems. Moreover, we fail to realize that the presence of an evil adversary at work in the world does not imply the absence of a good God.

Perhaps you've sent up prayers that seem to have gone unanswered. Maybe there's a longing deep in your heart that has yet to be satisfied. Circumstances that cause you to struggle with the idea that God is both fully sovereign and fully good. Believe me when I tell you that I get it. I've wrestled with these things too. And seasons may come when I'll wrestle with them again. But I can tell you, with the backing of Scripture and personal experience, that our Heavenly Father is unequivocally, and without a doubt, fully good and in control (see James 1:17; Psalm 111:7).

To really know and trust God in the way I'm talking about, we need to rethink Him apart from any preconceived, unbiblical ideas we might have picked up about Him. We have to be willing to put down any misconceptions we've adopted along the way and let God show us who He really is. Getting to know who He is, understanding His true nature and character, breaks down any barriers we have built up that keep us from the relationship God wants people to have with Him.

God desires an intimate, devoted relationship with each one of us. A relationship that satisfies our deepest needs and cultivates in us the family resemblance people were intended to bear. Such relationships are not developed by simply believing that God exists, by reciting facts about Him as if He were a historical figure like George Washington or the Queen of England, or by maintaining perfect church attendance. No. The way a person gets to know God is by approaching Him in the one way provided: each must place faith in His Son, Jesus Christ.

Before we enter into the upcoming chapters' discussion of what it means to embrace our identities as God's daughters, we need to lay some groundwork. In fact, let me start at the very beginning, at the foundational level of the Christian faith.

Humanity's story begins in the biblical book of Genesis. There we meet Creator God, who is holy and sinless. When He fashioned humans, He made us "very good" and without sin (Gen 1:31). Yet because God didn't want to place humans in the position of having no choice in whether or not to love Him in return, He gave us the gift of free will. We could *choose* whether or not to obey and love Him back. Sadly, Adam and Eve, the very first humans and our common ancestors, disobeyed God in the only way they could. They rejected Him as Father and rejected His love … with devastating results.

Because of their disobedience, all those within the human race are born sinners and are separated from God the Father (Romans 3:23). If given the same opportunity presented to Adam, we too would've chosen to rebel. In fact, we sin against Him in various ways all the time. Because of this, the Bible tells us that we are His enemies (Colossians 1:21). The penalty for our rebellion against Him is death, *eternal* separation from God and the blessings He's reserved for His children. But because God loves us so much, He made a way for us to be reconciled to Him (Romans 5:11).

The Bible makes this way of salvation very clear. Being reconciled to God begins with repentance. That's why Peter addressed the men in Israel this way: "Repent therefore, and turn back, that your sins may be blotted out" (Acts 3:19). To repent means more than being sorry for what you've done wrong. And it's not a singular experience. Instead, it denotes an ongoing change of mind about your sin that leads to a change of way. And while repentance is a much-neglected concept, it is a crucial aspect of genuine salvation. Without it we can't fully acknowledge our need for the Savior. Acknowledging that we are in a desperate situation spiritually and need someone to intervene with God for us is paramount because Jesus said, "I am the way, and the truth, and the life. No one comes to the Father except through me" (John 14:6).

God's Son Jesus didn't come to hang around with spiritually healthy people. He came as God's rescue plan for all people trapped in darkness. He wants nothing more than to cure the disease of sin in your life and mine. In confessing our sins and our need for Him as our Savior, we open ourselves to God's free gift of grace. When we do, our humbled hearts are ready to acknowledge that Jesus came to pay the price due for our sins, and that He did so by shedding His own blood on the cross (1 Corinthians 15:3; Colossians 1:20). But not only did Jesus take on the punishment that our sins earned. On the third day Christ rose from the grave, victorious over sin and death, so that we could be restored to a right relationship with God and be freed from the curse of death. Only through trusting in Christ's sacrifice and resurrection do people qualify to be called children of the Heavenly Father.

If, then, you haven't already done so, today is the perfect day to choose to offer your heart to God by putting your trust in His Son, Jesus. All you have to do is recognize that your sins offend the heart of God and separate you from Him, requiring the need for you to turn from them in repentance. Then confess your sins and your need for a Savior. Tell Jesus you want Him to be the Lord of your life and to show you how to live in a way that is pleasing to your Heavenly Father as you surrender your will to His. That's all it takes to become a child of God. So if you can't confidently call yourself God's daughter, go ahead and put the book down and tell God what's on your heart. I'll be right here waiting when you get back.

Maybe you asked Jesus into your heart years ago, yet still find yourself pulled into the same kind of wrong thinking that kept me feeling defeated for so long. That made it difficult for my daughter to tune out the world's lies about who she should be and how she should live.

Whether that's you, or whether you just now accepted Jesus as Savior, I pray this book will help you to start seeing yourself as God does.

As I sat on my couch years ago, thinking about my daughter and my own history of struggle, I felt compelled to find out for myself exactly what God said about who we are as His daughters. I wanted to know what my Heavenly Father had to say because I was convinced that only He would have the answers to set me—and all my sisters in the faith—free from the traps of self-doubt and low self-esteem.

Over the next several years, I pressed into God through studying His Word (the Bible), through spending time with Him in prayer, and by surrounding myself with godly friends who encouraged me and strengthened me in the faith. Slowly, I admitted to Him that while I longed to believe I was wanted, loved, forgiven, beautiful, and useful as His Word claims I am, I needed His help in facing down the many lies I had believed about myself and about Him. And as God revealed more of His truth, and as I chose to embrace it as such, those lies began to lose their grip on me. Not only did I begin to see myself as He does, but I began to see God for who He is. He is good, loving, kind, generous, holy, and merciful.

Because you and I accepted Jesus as Savior, we are God's children. We've received forgiveness of sins. Not only that, but we are set free from the power sin once had on our lives. As members of God's family, we cannot be separated from His love. We can find our identity in Him. And not only has He redeemed our lives here on earth, but God promises that a day is coming when He will wipe away every tear from our eyes and will welcome us into His presence forever! So, let's start thinking about ourselves from a biblical perspective. Let's see what God's Word says about us. Let's choose to be daring daughters of the Most High God. Dare to be moved, dare to be changed, and dare to become all that God wants us to be.

Get your Bible out and say this with me, sweet sister: "Here I am, Lord. Speak to me."

Chapter 1

You Are Chosen

"Even before he made the world,

God loved us and chose us in Christ to be holy

and without fault in his eyes."

Ephesians 1:4, NLT

I want you to take a trip down memory lane. I need you to go all the way back to middle school. Why in the world would I want you to do that? Who in their right mind wants to relive any part of it? After all, most think of the middle school experience as a tumultuous, uncertain, keep-my-head-down-till-I-get-out-of-here season of life. We don't typically remember the junior high years with general fondness, and that's exactly why I want us to go back there now. To get in touch with the kind of insecurity that's common to adolescence.

Mentally plunk yourself down right in the middle of gym class. Then imagine it's kickball day. If you didn't play kickball, then choose any day on which you had to play a sport that required teams. The coach has just picked two kids to be captains, and those girls are about to start their own selection process to determine who will be on their teams. As you stand in the sea of classmates, with breath held and fingers crossed, one single thought rolls over and over in your mind: *Please don't pick me last.* Being picked last would somehow bring with it that sickening feeling of being less worthy or wanted than your peers.

The desire to be chosen is innate. And if you have accepted Christ as your Savior, you need to realize that God actually chose *you* to be on His team. To be His daughter. Indeed, you have been hand-picked by the

Heavenly Father. This doesn't mean God looked down and picked you out of the crowd, like the team captain on kickball day. Rather, it means He chose to create you to fill a specific role in His family. Ephesians 1:4 says that this choosing took place before the foundation of the earth was laid. This leads me to believe that understanding what it means to be chosen by Him should be the foundation upon which we build our identities.

In our culture, being chosen largely depends on who we are—or on how others perceive us to be. Are we good enough, fast enough, pretty enough, smart enough? And even if we happen to be all of those things, will it really be enough? God's choosing of His children works differently. That He chose us has nothing to do with who we are, what we have done, or how good we have been. In fact, there was nothing we could do or say or be to be chosen. That we were selected for God's purposes before time began is simply and completely an act of God's immense and extraordinary love. It has nothing to do with us and everything to do with Him.

Amazingly, God knew all the sinful choices we would make and the paths we would take and the circumstances of our lives when He chose us. Nothing shocked God or caught Him off guard. He knew you would cheat on that test. He knew you would lie to your parents. He knew you would get too close to that boy. He knew. And yet He still chose you. He still wanted *you* on His team!

It shocks me to think that God knew about all the ways in which I would turn away from Him and all of my epic fails and short comings and still decided He wanted me to be His daughter. To be a part of the family tasked with practically sharing and proclaiming His love and truth in the world. It simply blows my mind.

The more I think on this idea of being chosen, the more clearly I see that it is actually God's character—and not our own—that should receive our focus here. Of course, there is no way I can encompass all that God is in one short chapter. Entire books and studies have been written that only scratch the surface of His majesty. His wisdom, glory, power, and goodness are part of an infinite greatness that our finite minds will never be able to fully comprehend this side of heaven. Our relationship with Him is a journey of constant unfolding as He reveals more about Himself to us over time. So, while my comments here will not be exhaustive, what I hope to do is to whet your spiritual palate just enough for you to "taste and see that the LORD is good" (Psalm 34:8) and that His choosing of you is a wonderful fact that should free you from feelings of being unwanted.

God Is Glorious

The psalmist beckons us to "magnify the LORD" (Psalm 34:3). In reflecting on Psalm 34 and what this means, pastor and author Eric J. Alexander writes, "When we magnify something we make its true nature more obvious and clearer to ourselves. ... The psalmist means ... that we are to make God more apparent to ourselves and others, and thus to develop a fuller awareness of the greatness and glory of His nature."[1] Indeed, there is no one like God. He's altogether glorious, magnificent, and deserving of our praise.

Throughout His Word, the Bible, God unveils His nature in part through the revelation of His many names, each one like a magnifying glass helping us better understand just how glorious He really is. By looking closely at these names and the circumstances in which God chose to reveal them, we begin to grasp the finer details of His divine attributes and, as Alexander wrote, develop a greater awareness of God's glory. So let's hold up our magnifying glasses so we can get a better look at the majesty of our Heavenly Father.

In Genesis 1:1 we see that the very first name by which God reveals Himself is *Elohim*, meaning Supreme God or Creator. The English term *God* is used to translate the name *Elohim* throughout the Old Testament. This is the perfect place to start because God's creation is one of the primary ways He chooses to reveal Himself to humankind; all the beautiful splendor of nature is meant to point us to God, who is far more grand and awe-inspiring than even the sum of all He's made. In Psalm 19:1 we are told that "the heavens declare the glory of God," and in Romans 1:19 we find assurance that what can be known about God is shown to us through His creation. That's why the prophet could say in Isaiah 6:3 that "the whole earth is full of his glory." His "invisible attributes, namely, his eternal power and divine nature, have been clearly perceived, ever since the creation of the world, in the things that have been made" (Romans 1:20).

Beyond the sheer beauty of creation lies an intricate design, a design so precise and perfected that it speaks volumes of the One who created it. His character is seen in the particularity of His creation. For instance, clearly He is sovereign over creation because He's given meticulous attention to things as small as the complex workings within single cells. God's desire for intimacy with that which He created is revealed in His attention to detail. Only someone with tremendous care for his beloved would go to such lengths to perfect even the minutest element of his workmanship.

God's choice of us isn't about how great we are but how amazing He is (Psalm 8:3-4). To understand just how extraordinary it is that God wants a relationship with us, we first must understand how small we are in comparison to His majesty. Too often we conform God to something to which we can relate. We reduce His boundlessness to fit within our own limited framework of understanding. But Isaiah wrote, "Who [but God] has measured the waters in the hollow of his hand and marked off the heavens with a span, enclosed the dust of the earth in a measure and weighed the mountains in scales and the hills in a balance?" (Isaiah 40:12).

To gain a better perspective on just how incredible it is that God even notices us, not to mention chooses us, we have to consider how big the universe really is.[2] For starters, imagine our sun being the size of a penny. If you laid that penny on the ground, the nearest star would be about 350 miles away from it! Moreover, did you know that researchers have concluded that nearly every star in the universe has at least one planet orbiting it—just as the planets orbit the sun in our solar system? Not only that, but scientists estimate there are between two-hundred-billion and four-hundred-billion stars in our galaxy alone, which translates to somewhere between three and ten-trillion planets existing within just the Milky Way. There are at least two-hundred-billion galaxies in the known universe, which means there are about one-septillion planets out there. That's a one with twenty-four zeros behind it.[3] And that's a *gigantic* universe!

Frankly, I can't even begin to wrap my mind around something that expansive. And you too probably suffer with tunnel vision because the human perception of reality tends to be consumed by the modest portion of it that is our everyday lives. It's as if we block from our peripheral vision the things that seem too big for us to comprehend.

We have to work to push through that tendency. For now, let's scale our view of the universe down just a bit so that we can focus more closely on the little blue planet we call home. Did you know that over two hundred known parameters have to come together perfectly for any planet to be able to sustain life?[4] And earth is the only known planet to have met those parameters in their entirety. More amazing is that the number of known, required parameters continues to increase as scientists make new discoveries, significantly narrowing the possibility of there being any other planet with the ability to sustain life.

Just think about the many things that work in synergistic harmony, keeping tempo for the delicate, intricate dance of life to happen. The pull of the other planets in our solar system, for instance, helps keep the earth in its orbit. The gravitational pull of the moon helps prevent meteors from crashing into our atmosphere. The precise ratio of oxygen in our atmosphere, the tilt of the earth's axis, and our distance from the sun were all carefully planned out by our Creator so that life on earth can exist. And all of these factors, every single one of them, must remain constant if life here is to continue. Intricate and intentional attention to detail is what made creation possible and God's continuing, careful watch is what allows life to go on.

Here are some more details that blow me away. Did you know there are more than 1.4 million different kinds of creatures living on our tiny planet? Indeed, it's as Isaiah 45:18 says: "The Creator of the heavens, the God who formed the earth and made it, the one who established it (he did not create it to be a wasteland, but formed it to be inhabited)." But out of all those creatures in their vast array, there is only one of which God said, "Let us make man in our image, after our likeness" (Genesis 1:26). Think of that! There is no other creature in this world, in our solar system, or in the entire ninety-three-billion light-year-wide universe that can claim that.[5] God chose us— frail, fragile, finite human beings—to look like Him, partner with Him in His work, and have the ability to live in fellowship with Him. Talk about exclusive!

I'm hopeful that these realities will help you embrace just how special you are to your Heavenly Father. The preciseness and beauty and majesty of God's creation all testify to His eternal power and divine nature so that we can grasp just how glorious He is (Romans 1:20). But the care He took in His design for life, the artistry and the detail, they all speak of something else too. They shout of His genuine concern for His beloved creation: you!

As I think on this, I want to cry out as King David did:

> *"Blessed are you, O Lord, ... Yours, O Lord, is the greatness and the power and the glory and the victory and the majesty, for all that is in the heavens and in the earth is yours. Yours is the kingdom, O Lord, and you are exalted as head above all. ... In your hand are power and might, and in your hand it is to make great and to give strength to all. And now [I] thank you, our God, and praise your glorious name"* (1 Chronicles 29:10-13).

May you and I never grow immune to the amazing reality that the Creator of the universe, who calls each of those billions of stars by name, knows how many hairs are on our heads (Luke 12:7). The One who spoke the world into being longs to speak to our hearts (Hebrews 1:1-2). He desires relationship with us (James 4:8). Know that He considers you worthy, sweet sister. You are wanted!

God Is Ever Aware

Before I tell you the next name we're going to ponder together, I want to give you a backstory. What we're about to discover is one of my favorite names by which God reveals Himself, but to grasp the fullness of it, we need to have some context.

Farther into the book of Genesis, the same book in which God first identifies Himself as Creator, we encounter the story of a woman named Hagar. Hagar was the maidservant of Abram's wife Sarai. And if those names don't sound familiar to you, know that the latter pair was later renamed Abraham and Sarah. When Sarai realized she was unable to have children of her own, she decided to give her maidservant to Abram so that he might have a child through her (Genesis 16:1-4).

Clearly this plan was a recipe for disaster. Sarai not only gave her husband permission to take another wife, but she encouraged it! It helps to know, though, that it was common practice in Middle Eastern culture of that time for unfertile wives to provide their maidservants to their husbands. In such cases, a maidservant's baby could be considered as belonging to her mistress rather than herself and would therefore be entitled to the full inheritance as the father's heir. This form of surrogacy was widely accepted during this period; nevertheless, it caused all kinds of family drama.

Importantly, ten years prior to this incident involving Hagar, God had given Abram a promise that his offspring would be as numerous as the stars (Genesis 15:5). But when a whole decade passed and Sarai still hadn't borne Abram any children, she became discouraged and doubted God's ability and desire to fulfill His promise through her. After all, she'd reached her mid-seventies and Abram was somewhere around eighty-five (Genesis 16:16). So Sarai allowed the improbability of her circumstance to overshadow her faith in the power of God. That's why she decided to take matters into her own hands, coming up with what she thought was a good Plan B.

Can you relate to her feelings of desperation? I know I can. They tend to come when we know what God promises in His Word and what He has spoken to our hearts, but either time or circumstances have caused us to doubt. We start to wonder, *Did God really say that?* or *Has God changed His mind?* And as we dwell on those questions rather than on God's faithfulness, we start to feel like God has forgotten about us altogether. We must realize that it was just that kind of thinking that led Sarai to talk her husband into having a child with another woman.

Hagar did indeed become pregnant, with disastrous results. Abram's child grew in her womb during a time in history when a woman's inability to have children was considered a divine punishment. The Bible, in fact, gives us several examples of women being chastised and ridiculed because of their infertility (see Genesis 30:1-13; 1 Samuel 1:4-7; Luke 1:8-25). Such abuse was never condoned by God. Nevertheless, Sarai too found herself dealing with such bullying. Hagar didn't just look down on Sarai; she began to despise her. The Bible says that Hagar "looked with contempt on her mistress" (Genesis 16:4).

Hagar's attitude must have compounded the feelings Sarai already struggled with. Feelings of unworthiness, of hopelessness, of anger, and of shame. And I don't think we should miss that she essentially put herself through a lot of additional grief because she doubted the value and purpose God had already placed on her, both when He created her and when He chose her for the job of being matriarch to the Jewish people—a reality she could only take on faith at that time. Sadly, the way the world judged her circumstance became the measuring stick by which she defined her worth.

It wasn't long before Sarai began to treat Hagar harshly. So harshly, in fact, that Hagar ran away. I can only imagine the thoughts that were going through her

27

mind as she fled into the wilderness: *I didn't ask to marry Abram. It's not my fault Sarai couldn't get pregnant. Where will I go now?* It's apparent from the text that as Hagar fled into the desert, she was indeed unsure where to go. After all, she was the foreign maidservant of a Hebrew family. She was far from her native Egypt and fleeing from the camp she'd called home. She had no plan. No safe place. And no means to get there even if she did. The poor girl was alone—or so she thought.

It was in the midst of Hagar's tragic situation that God showed up to reveal Himself by one of my favorite names. Right there in the desert, the angel of the LORD— which is to be understood as a reference to the preincarnate Christ—approached Hagar, spoke a blessing over her, and even revealed details about the child she carried.

As a result of this encounter, Hagar said of the Lord, "'You are a God of seeing' for she said, 'Truly I have seen him who looks after me'" (Genesis 16:13). In Hebrew, the name Hagar applies here is *El Roi*; it means the God who Sees. The word *roi* means to look upon and have regard for, to behold, to be near. God *saw* Hagar. He saw her misery; He saw her need; and He saw her future. He didn't just look in her direction or happen to notice her. God wasn't watching from a distance like a spectator; rather, He observed her as someone who is intimately involved in the situation, as someone who is personally invested in the outcome. And God showed Hagar just how close He was to her. He let her see that she was not alone.

God sees you too, sweet sister. His eyes are fixed on you. Just as a doting father sits captivated, watching his precious daughter play and grow and learn, so your Heavenly Father watches over you. And as sure as God revealed His nearness to Hagar in her time of need, He longs to reveal Himself to you.

Our Father chooses many ways to reveal Himself to His daughters. Sometimes it's through the words of a friend, or even a stranger. He may speak through His provision in circumstances or an answer to prayer. And there will be times when God chooses to speak directly to our hearts. But the Bible is His Word, and it's meant to speak to us every time we open its pages.

God desires to show you that you have a purpose. He created you with your future in mind. It's a future full of hope and meaning (Jeremiah 29:11). So if you feel like Sarai and wonder if God has forgotten you or better identify with Hagar and feel completely alone, be assured that God sees your heart. He knows your need. He cares deeply for you. And as He did for Hagar, He can speak hope into your darkness.

God is Our Abba Father

Before closing this chapter, I want us to give close attention to one more of God's names—a name I mentioned briefly in the introduction because it appears in the title of this book. This name is *Abba*, the Aramaic name for Father. It is through Jesus, God's Son, that His role as our Abba is revealed (Luke 10:22). Although throughout the Old Testament God is referred to as the Father of His people, Jesus invited His followers to an even more personal, more intimate relationship with their Heavenly Father. Indeed, while God remains the patriarchal ruler of His people and is still deserving of our reverence as such, Jesus paints for us the picture of God as a Daddy who is approachable and near.

To better see God in this light, we should first take a close look at His relationship with His only begotten Son, Jesus. Importantly, Jesus—like God—has always existed. However, we read in Luke 2 about how He came in the form of a human baby in order to become the perfect sacrifice for man's sin. And just like an expectant dad of today who sends out blithesome announcements as his child's birth approaches, God would not let the big event go unnoticed. Having planned Christ's arrival before the dawn of time, in fact, He'd been announcing His coming through the prophets for thousands of years (Isaiah 7:14; Zechariah 9:9; Micah 5:2; Daniel 7:13-14) long before He let Mary and Joseph in on the surprise. Just telling a few wasn't enough for this proud Poppa, though. He wanted to let people know it was time to celebrate!

The celebration was so great that heaven could not contain it. A new star shone brightly in the sky, prompting wise men from the east to set out in pursuit of the Messiah. Then, as Jesus entered the world, the party spilled out of the heavens right on top of some poor, unsuspecting shepherds who were just trying to keep up with their sheep (Luke 2:8-9). Just imagine it! Angels from heaven came down to earth singing, "Glory to God in the highest!" as Mary placed Jesus in a manger (Luke 2:13-14). (Oh, to actually hear angels sing. Now that's something I'm really looking forward to experiencing in heaven!)

Please don't miss this. When His Son Jesus was born, God sent an angelic choir to sing about it. But Zephaniah 3:17 tells us that God, our Abba Father, personally rejoices over *us* with singing! And as if that isn't amazing enough, know that the angels in heaven too sang out in their joy over you when you accepted Christ and became God's daughter (Luke 15:10)! Your spiritual birth caused an angelic party. As sure as He rejoiced over the coming of Jesus, Abba Father adores you.

In this book about seeing God as our Abba, I think it's important to pause here for a moment to talk about a difficult reality. Being chosen by God is a wonderful thing. But it will not exempt us from hardship in the world.

Consider what Jesus endured. He came as God in the flesh. He was perfect! Yet even those who walked with Jesus, who claimed not only to believe in Him but to love Him, abandoned Him at His time of greatest need. And this fallen world, full of sin and evil, rejected Him. People even tortured Him and nailed Him to a cross.

The world's unbelief, their rejection, however, did not diminish Jesus's worth. Thus, His eyes kept their focus on the fulfillment of God's plan, not on the temporary distractions of the day. He knew that His purpose was not to go get cozy with this world but to do the will of His Father (Matthew 7:21). And though the Son faced many hardships, it did not change the fact that God is a good, good Father.

It can be hard at times to believe that God is good, especially when we are struggling with crisis or trauma or loss. I'm not going to lie: I have cried out to God from the depths of my brokenness wondering why God would allow hardship to fall on His servant. I've asked things like, *Where is God's light in the midst of my season of darkness? When will that peace He promises finally penetrate my aching heart?* Don't feel that you are alone if you have ever asked those questions. And don't feel like you're going to alienate or anger God if you do. He's big enough to handle our emotions, even when we feel like those emotions just might break us.

As Jesus hung on the cross, struggling just to take a breath, suffering the most unbearable anguish for crimes He didn't commit, He cried out, "My God, my God, why have you forsaken me?" (Matthew 27:46). And that heartbreaking cry tells us that in His final moments, even Jesus felt utterly abandoned by His Abba Father. Nevertheless, He knew that feelings must not have the last word. How do I know? Because the next words He spoke, which totally wreck me, were these: "Father, into your hands I commit my spirit" (Luke 23:46).

These words challenge me and convict me and give me such hope! In the midst of utter torment, Jesus chose to trust the goodness of His Abba over the cruelty of this world.

Thankfully, most of us will never be called to endure such suffering. But as God's children, we are called to pick up our cross—whatever it might look like— and follow Him (Matthew 16:24). Therefore, we must put down our selfish desires for lifetimes of only smooth sailing and pursue the heart of our heavenly Father.

You have been chosen by the Creator of the universe, who loves you with an everlasting love

(Jeremiah 31:3). He watches over you with deep concern and adoration. Not one thing comes into your life that does not first pass thorough His sovereign hands. All of it, whether good or bad, in fact, can all be used by God for your good and His glory (Romans 8:28). He will be your strength to face it. And when everything is said and done, you will stand in His eternal presence, in the perfection of His intended vision for you, His precious, beloved daughter.

Jesus assures us that we have a loving Father who will take care of us. All we need to do is seek His will, knowing He will provide everything we need whatever we may face (Matthew 6:33).

Questions for Group or Personal Reflection

1. Tell about a specific situation that helps you identify with the feeling of not being wanted.

   Childhood

2. How does it make you feel to know that nothing about you is hidden from God, yet He still wants you to be His daughter? How does this knowledge change the way you think about God? *Loved beyond - makes me feel close & accepted that He wants a relationship*

3. How does nature help expand your view of God? *Wow! To see God in all - He is not a little God! Even the birds proclaim Him.*

4. What does Jesus's trust in, obedience to, and dependence upon God teach about what our response to our Heavenly Father should be?

   The same: trust, obey and depend.

Chapter 2

You Are Loved

"I pray that you, being rooted and firmly established

in love, may be able to comprehend with all the

saints what is the length and width,

height and depth of God's love, and to know

Christ's love that surpasses knowledge, so that you

may be filled with all the fullness of God."

Ephesians 3:17-19, CSB

Jessie + Emily

I tried for years to wrap my head around Ephesians 3:17-19, which is printed on the opening page of this chapter, desperate to know a love that I just couldn't understand. Trying to comprehend that God really loves me wholeheartedly was like trying to grasp the concept of astrophysics or the space-time continuum. The concept was way above my intellectual abilities, for sure! I didn't understand how I ever could grasp something that seemed so mind-blowing.

True to form, though, I was making a biblical truth much harder than it needed to be. And true to the way God often deals with me, He waited for me to stop trying to figure it out myself and to actually ask Him for the answer.

It turned out that much of the reason God's abundant love for me was such a tough thing for me to process was that in our humanness, "love" is easily misunderstood and rather selfishly defined. We love our parents because they take care of us. We love food because it tastes yummy. We love our husbands because they treat us well. We love a movie because it entertains us. What we call love is generally extended only because of what someone or something does for us.

By contrast, God's kind of love is given without such self-centered reasoning. God loved us before we were born (Psalm 139:16). He loved us before we loved Him (Romans 5:8). And He still loves us even in the times when we are not so easy to love (Romans 8:35-39). His brand of love—divine love—is expressed in His faithful provision for His people throughout all generations. It is evidenced in the beauty of nature in that everywhere we look, in every sunrise, in every season, in every part of creation we are reminded of just how great His thoughts are toward us. It was made tangible in the life, sacrificial death, and resurrection of His Son Jesus. And it continues to be seen in His relentless pursuit of His most beloved creation, humankind, whom He longs to have with Him forever.

Though we may not fully understand such a love, we can learn to trust it. To do so, we need to grasp that the kind of love of which Scripture speaks most often is far superior to the many uses of the term that are common to English language speakers. We use the word "love" to describe how we feel about everything from marriage to ice cream to puppy dogs. The term is generalized and gets used in all kinds of insincere applications. But did you know that this one English word has been used in place of over twenty different words for love and their variants in the Hebrew and Greek texts of the Bible?[6] It's no wonder we have a hard time believing in or understanding the unconditional, irrational, unending love of God! We struggle to grasp that it's anymore pure and meaningful than the fleeting, shallow love we express for a pair of really cute shoes.

God Is Love Itself

In the book of 1 John we get an expository lesson on the love of God—its height, depth, and breadth—and the importance of God's children remaining in that love. The writer of the book was John, who is also known as the Beloved Disciple. I believe he was gifted with a special ability to know the richness of God's affection in a way most of us miss in part because he literally walked alongside Jesus for three years. It is out of his intimate knowledge that John was able to reveal to us God's love in a way that we can understand.

John declared the boundlessness of God's love when he said, "In this is love, not that we have loved God but that he loved us and sent his Son to be the propitiation for our sins" (1 John 4:10). When I read John's words, written nearly two-thousand years ago, I can almost see God's love for us spilling onto the pages before him through his pen. Remarkably, he assured us that not only does God love us but that He *is* love (1 John 4:8). Think about that! Everything God does, says, purposes, and plans is rooted in the love He embodies. I really like the way Timothy R. Jennings explains it in his book, *The God-Shaped Brain*:

> "The core, central, primary characteristic of God ... is love (1Jn 4:8). Not the silly, finite,

flimsy, emotional, wax-fruit imposter we sometimes call love, but a boundless, eternal, bottomless, never-ending, reality of goodness on which the cosmos is built! A love that lasts, that creates, that is constant.

"God is love. The Bible does not say God *is* forgiveness, even though he is forgiving; or that God *is* knowledge, even though he is all-knowing; or that God *is* power, even though he is all-powerful. All other attributes are, like facets on a diamond, radiant windows into the heart of God. But with regard to love, God does not merely act it out—he embodies it!"[7]

As I consider this beautiful truth and recall Paul's prayer in Ephesians 3:17-19, I find myself growing in certainty that God wants to take His people up out of the spiritual desert lands in which many have lived for so long to transplant us into a place where our roots can go deep. What I mean is that our lives, our hearts, need to be deeply interwoven in the soil of the love of God our Father. Only then can we truly draw up the nourishment of God's provision like water from a stream. Tapping into His love strengthens our spiritual foundation. And the stronger our foundation becomes, the more God can fill us with His fullness so that we might be able to comprehend the love of Christ more completely. And the better we are able to comprehend Christ's love, the more that love will heal, restore, and change our hearts. And overflow into the lives of those around us.

Qualities of True Love

The surrounding culture teaches that love for others is tolerant, passive, and self-serving. It's also considered conditional, is based on shifting emotions, and ends as soon as we don't feel like loving anymore. These days it's as easy as the click of a button to unfriend people on social media. There's even a billboard in my town that echoes loudly our culture's lack of relational commitment on an even more disturbing level, advertising a certain lawyer's "$199 divorce special." We've become much more concerned with how we feel than with how we might heal, which has led to a general cheapening of the concept of love.

Because we are bombarded with this counterfeit version of love, simply knowing that God's love for us is eternal and unchanging won't produce a lasting change in us. We need to understand more specifically what God's brand of love is and what it's not. Let's look at what 1 Corinthians 13 has to say:

> *"Love is patient, love is kind. It does not envy, it does not boast, it is not proud. It*

does not dishonor others, it is not self-seeking, it is not easily angered, it keeps no record of wrongs. Love does not delight in evil but rejoices with the truth. It always protects, always trusts, always hopes, always perseveres. Love never fails." (1 Corinthians 13:4-8, NIV)

Let's break this Scripture down together and look at each of these qualities more closely. It's going to help us get the foundation we need to produce lasting change.

Right out of the gate, we see that real love is actually patient and kind. These two realities, in fact, go hand-in-hand. To be patient means to endure, to wait for. Some Bible translations use the term "long-suffering" to get at this concept. Either implies that love is not necessarily comfortable nor enjoyable for the one who is doing the waiting. To be kind means to be useful or charitable, to act benevolently and graciously. Really loving, then, means being aware of the needs of those around you and seeking to alleviate suffering when you are able. And, when you can't alleviate suffering, you still do what you can to provide comfort in it.

The idea that love is patient and kind isn't meant to produce warm fuzzy feelings. It is intended to remind us that rather than growing impatient or frustrated, the one who truly loves actively seeks out ways to help, encourage, or otherwise benefit others.

God showed you and me this kind of love in that "while we were still sinners, Christ died for us" (Romans 5:8). He didn't passively sit back and wait until we were worth saving. He didn't hold off until we deserved help. Rather, God actively provided the way for our salvation. He sent Christ, who died freely for all who'd believe. And the grace offered through Him is a gift with no strings attached (Romans 3:22-24). There is no greater love than that of one who would die for his friends (John 15:13). Jesus laid down His life for you, dear one. God sent His own Son to die on the cross so that you and I might live. That is true love. That is the kind of amazing, self-sacrificing love the Father has for all His beloved children.

When we truly begin to comprehend and embrace the kind of love God has for us, it changes us. In fact, as we accept the love that God pours into our hearts, we soon find that He doesn't stop pouring once a heart is full. He keeps pouring so that His love might overflow out of us and into the lives of those around us. It's because of this truth that Jesus said, "Just as I have loved you, you are also to love one another. By this all people will know that you are my disciples" (John 13:34-35).

The original Greek word for love used in 1 Corinthians 13 is *agape*. *Vine's Complete Expository Dictionary* defines it as "The deep and constant love and interest of a perfect Being (God) towards entirely unworthy objects, producing and fostering a reverential love in them towards the Giver, and a practical love towards those who are partakers of the same, and a desire to help others to seek the Giver."[8] It goes on to say that this love "can be known only from the actions it prompts."[9] I'm sure you've heard it said that the proof is in the pudding. Well, this is where the proof and the pudding come together for the children of God: true love and loving actions are partners.

To see how this principle should play out in our lives, let's dig a little deeper into 1 Corinthians 13. Verse 4 says love "does not envy" (NIV). Envy is a monster with the potential to destroy relationships and lives. Its desires are selfish; it gets upset when someone else gets what it wants. Envy stems from a belief that we somehow deserve something more than others do. And it leads to bitterness, resentment, and entitlement. God knew this when He told us not to covet our neighbors' stuff (Exodus 20:17). He was warning us of the dangers and potential damage envy can cause when we allow it to take root in our hearts.

If we are to love others as God loves us, we mustn't envy. Instead, we need to get excited about the good fortune of others, even when we don't get to partake in their blessings. As I consider this concept, I'm reminded of *The Great British Baking Show*, which I so enjoy. It's really fun to watch. One of the reasons I like it is because of the dry sense of humor the hosts interject into every show. But another reason I do—and the reason that's most pertinent to this discussion—is that the show's contestants demonstrate genuine affection for one another. Though they are in competition, they celebrate each other's victories and even cry over eliminations. They seem to exemplify the sort of humble winning and gracious losing that is lacking in much of society, but that should be common among those who have been adopted into God's family.

In Philippians 4:12-13 the apostle Paul notes that he found the secret to defeating that monster called envy: contentment in Christ. To him, the comforts of this world were little more than a distraction because he knew where his real treasure lay. When we recognize the depth of God's love for us and seek to love Him in return, we too will find that our own treasure is in heaven: in spending eternity with our Heavenly Father. And doing so makes us far less vulnerable to the temptation to envy.

Before I leave this topic, I must point out that envy is the close relative of boasting and pride. They are two sides of the same coin, which may be why they are mentioned together in 1 Corinthians 13:4. Where envy is angry about what others have that it does not, pride gets puffed up and brags about what it has that others don't. Pride exalts itself above others and enjoys rubbing things in their faces. Boasting puts others down in an attempt to make oneself feel superior. Though assuring ourselves that we are better off than those around us can temporarily satisfy our carnal desires, such an attitude in no way reflects biblical love.

Paul's mission, the thing that got him out of bed every day, was the desire to complete the work God had given him to do—to testify to the gospel of the grace of God (Acts 20:24). No earthly accolade, no material thing, no opportunity could outshine the joy he felt at the thought of hearing his Heavenly Father say, "Well done" upon his entrance into heaven (Matthew 25:23). And no worldly pleasure could satisfy him half as well as seeing a life redeemed by the power of Christ (1 Corinthians 9:22-23).

If you want to defeat a tendency toward envy, boasting, or pride in your life, remember that drawing people into His family is the ultimate goal of God's love. To add to our group others who are being saved. To look beyond our own concerns to reach out and meet the needs of those around us so that they might get a glimpse of God's love for them.

Interestingly, it was just this kind of love in action that drew me toward God. Though the Lord saw me at my ugliest, He drew me to Himself by seeing my need for agape love and filling it. He brought me into a community of other women who were His daughters, a group of ladies who lived like those earliest Christian believers who are described in Acts 2:44-46. They would eat at each other's homes, go to church together, and practically meet each other's needs however they were able. I had never been part of a community like that before, and it changed my life. It made me crave Jesus. And that is the objective of agape love.

Just think how many marriages could be saved, how many hungry tummies could be fed, how many jail cells could be emptied if we made a lifestyle of seeking out ways to meet the emotional, physical, and spiritual needs of others with the love of God. True, it takes intentional dedication to love others well. To fight for, wait for, and work hard for their benefit. But it is always worth it—even when it doesn't feel like it.

Another quality that sets agape love apart from lesser understandings of love is that it is not easily angered. If you think about it, anger generally comes out when we feel we've been wronged in some way—when someone was mean to us or offended us or took something from us. And frankly, anger often comes when we feel like others aren't showing love toward us.

I, for example, don't get angry very frequently, but when I do it's often aimed toward those I claim to love the most: my family. Sometimes I lose my temper when my son keeps forgetting to do the thing I've asked him to do a hundred times. Or when my daughter forgets to tell me her plans have changed, and it forces me to change the plans I've made to accommodate her. Or when my husband and I are disagreeing about something, and he refuses to see my point of view. When these things happen, I don't feel loved by them. And sadly, I don't always respond in a way that makes them feel loved by me. Perhaps you can relate.

Whatever the case may be, Dr. Marcus Dods provides a helpful insight that we'll do well to remember. He says,

> "Love is not fired up with resentment at every slight, and does not make a mental note and lay up in its memory the contempt shown by one, the indifference shown by another, the intention to wound by a third. Love is too little occupied with itself to feel these exhibitions of malice very keenly. It is bent on winning the battle for others, and the wounds received in the cause are made

light of. Its eye is on the advantage to be gained by the needy, and not on itself."[10]

When we feel like we're not being loved well by others, we tend to retaliate. To defend ourselves. That's a very natural human reaction. But it's not the appropriate reaction for Abba's daughters. It doesn't reflect God's heart. When I read Dr. Dods' description of love, it really convicts me. How often am I so concerned with myself that I go blind to the needs of others? I'm not sure I want to answer that question, but I do think a candid response to it can reveal a lot about whether I'm loving people the way God does. The way I, as His daughter, should.

Consider the story of the Good Samaritan in Luke 10. Jews and Samaritans were by all accounts enemies. This animosity dates back to the time of the divided kingdom, when pagans imported into Israel by a conquering king in 721 BC intermingled their own beliefs with traditional Jewish religion. By Jesus's day, the two people groups disliked each other so much that Jews would travel one or two days out of their way just to avoid having to go through the land that came to be called Samaria. (Have you ever gone out of your way to avoid seeing someone you didn't like? I'll regretfully admit that I have.)

In Jesus's story he tells of a Samaritan man who came across a Jew who had been beaten and left for dead on the side of the road. A priest and a Levite (Jews themselves) had already passed this man by, leaving him there to suffer (Luke 10:31-32). Apparently it was too much of an inconvenience for either of them to stop and help. But when the Samaritan, the beaten traveler's national enemy, came along, he was moved with compassion for him (Luke 10:33). And rather than avoiding him like the other men did, the Samaritan went out of his way to help him. He not only bound up his wounds there on the road, but proceeded to take him to the nearest village where he secured and paid for his medical care (Luke 10:34-35).

The Samaritan didn't see an enemy. He didn't see an inconvenience. He saw a need. He chose to lay aside any contempt he might have felt to show compassion instead. That is the kind of true love the Bible teaches us to embrace. It's the kind God shows us! That is genuine, Holy Spirit empowered, agape love. It reflects a choice not to count someone as an enemy but to take advantage of opportunities to battle against the things that divide us. To see that others are just as in need of mercy and love as we are.

When you read the 1 Corinthians 13 passage, you may have found yourself wondering, what "love does not delight in evil but rejoices with the truth" means. Let me tell you what God showed me. In short, it means that true love doesn't just turn a blind eye when someone is headed down a dangerous, sinful road; rather, love warns of trouble ahead and rejoices when the truth of God's Word is embraced instead. Of course, in this current culture that prides itself on tolerance, applying the kind of tough love to which this passage refers can often do more than just ruffle a few feathers. It can be mistaken for hate. In an age of relativism in which evil is celebrated and truth is subjective, walking this out takes prayerful balance.

Balance is only achieved when truth and love walk in unity. Take one without the other and they both lose their effectiveness. If, for example, you say you love someone by meeting a practical need but refuse to share the truth of God's Word regarding sin and what Jesus came to do about it, you are withholding the fullness of God's majesty and redemption. If you speak the truth without clothing it in the grace and love we have been given in Christ, it will only serve to condemn those who hear.

A dear friend of mine has lived a homosexual lifestyle for many years now. She and her partner have been together longer than my husband and I have been married. And both of them are funny, kind, and wonderful people whom we love dearly. Nevertheless, we do not agree with their relationship, and they both know why.

When they held a wedding ceremony a few years ago, my husband and I did not attend. As much as we love our friends, we could not celebrate their sin. We could not compromise the truth of God's Word regarding sexual immorality and the biblical design for marriage. Importantly, though, we haven't disowned them or cut off our relationship with them. And we don't shove what we believe down their throats every time we see them. Since they know what we believe and what the Bible says, we don't need to keep reminding them. Rather, it's our job to share with them the truth of God's love consistently through action. And as we do, we trust that it's only the Holy Spirit who can convict their hearts and help them see their need for Jesus.

If we had not made clear to them what God says about sexual sin, we would have been neglecting the truth of God's Word. If we suddenly cut them off from our friendship, we would not be showing them the extent of God's love and compassion that are found in Christ. Just loving them without sharing God's truth or sharing the truth apart from welcoming them with God's love would only serve to drive them further into a culture that celebrates and encourages their choices. Our job is to love them in such a way that they are drawn to Jesus because only Jesus can change their hearts.

I chose to share this story not to point a finger at homosexuality—after all, it's no more sinful than adultery or heterosexual fornication. Instead, I chose it to draw attention to the fact that we cannot condone any act of willful sin if we expect those with whom we come in contact to see their need for the Savior. The holiness of our Creator demands that we acknowledge the depravity of all sin and the consequence of willfully choosing a sinful lifestyle. To do less would be unloving.

When I first came to the phrase "love protects" in 1 Corinthians 13:7, I had to stop for a minute to process the many visuals swirling in my mind. Some of them were vibrant pictures of what protective love looks like; others were rather disturbing images of the counterfeit loves we can so easily buy into.

Before meeting my amazing husband, I had a few relationships that were less than protective. I had dated men who lied to me, hurt me, used me, and left me to fend for myself. Somehow I justified their actions as love because I didn't know that it wasn't. I thought that if they said they loved me, their claims must be true—even if their actions didn't support that. And I've fallen into the same tendency when dealing with "friends."

Perhaps you find yourself thinking about relationships as I once did, either not knowing or not believing that you deserve any better than to be wounded by the selfish, so-called love that's so prevalent in our world. Dear friend, please hear me. The Word of God says "love protects." The Greek word for protect in this verse is *stegrō*. It means to roof over, cover with silence, to suffer.[11] This tells us that true love serves to defend like a roof sheltering the object of its affections. And it doesn't just shelter but takes upon itself the beating of the storms that threaten its beloved. Moreover, love doesn't complain or try to induce guilt or a sense of indebtedness for any suffering it incurs. You are God's beloved, and He is your shelter. David expressed his confidence in this truth when he penned these words in Psalm 18:2: "You are my mighty rock, my fortress, my protector, the rock where I am safe, my shield, my powerful weapon, and my place of shelter" (CEV). The definition of *stegrō* provides us the pattern that all truly loving relationships follow.

I did not grow up with a firm sense that I was protected by anyone. I don't mean to suggest that my parents neglected me, but my sense of safety was shaken due to some traumatic events. Therefore, learning to trust God as my place of safety has been transforming for me. It has unlocked the secrets to His peace and joy and enabled me to find courage where otherwise I would have none. He is the place I run to when I am tired, scared, sad, or overwhelmed. And without fail, when I run to Him, I find comfort, help, and rest. My circumstances might not immediately change, my problems may not disappear, but I do find the help and strength to face them and the hope that I will get through them. That's why I say with the psalmist, "Let all who take refuge in you rejoice [God]; let them sing joyful praises forever. Spread your protection over them, that all who love your name may be filled with joy. For you bless the godly, O LORD; you surround them with your shield of love" (Psalm 5:11-12, NLT).

First Corinthians 13 assures us that true love always trusts, has faith, and believes the best. It always hopes, expects, and anticipates that good will win. Love perseveres, remains, and endures even and especially when times get tough. It never fails, falls away, or becomes inefficient. Why? Because it isn't based on fleeting emotions but is a deliberate act of the will.

Our love for others will prove to be flawed. We will make mistakes and drop the ball and come up short as we try to emulate the kind of love God embodies. But we can try. And we can trust that no matter how imperfect our love may appear, God's love for us is perfect and complete.

Before we wrap up this chapter, I'd like to tell you a story. It's about a man I know who was totally in love with a particular girl. As far as he was concerned, she was beautiful, smart, and the whole package. He adored her at first sight, and he knew he'd be in love with her forever.

Initially, the girl noticed the man hanging around her but paid little attention to him. His feelings for her were pretty obvious; he didn't hide them well! But, she felt he wasn't really her type. She preferred a hunky bad-boy to this quiet, sensitive guy.

Over time, however, the two did eventually become friends. She found that he was easy to talk to. In fact, he offered surprisingly insightful advice when one bad-boy she'd chosen broke her heart. Nevertheless, she didn't take the advice. And it wasn't long before she began seeing another bad boy who would also leave her heart in pieces. It set a pattern that soon became a habit.

Though the guy who really loved the girl wanted to help her, he eventually had to distance himself from her as she continued walking down the road she'd chosen. He knew that she had some tough lessons to learn. And because he knew her so well, he realized that the best thing he could do was let her learn them the hard way. (Sometimes when speaking the truth in love doesn't work, that's all you can do.)

A few years passed and the girl found herself in a really bad place. After a succession of unhealthy relationships ended in break ups, she realized that things in her life had gone terribly wrong and she didn't know how to turn them around. She'd started to think that there was something wrong with her, some kind of flaw that made her unworthy of love. In truth, she'd been trying to find love from guys who would never be able to give it. As a result, she'd made some pretty bad choices that led her to an emotionally dark place with no clear path out.

One summer day as she was sitting in her car at a stoplight, she began to think. It was miserably hot and suffocatingly humid. The lack of air conditioning and the fact that the car had only one working window seemed to echo the hopelessness she felt. Life had gotten overwhelming. She was frightened by her outlook. She felt dreadfully alone. The girl was longing for a place of comfort, a refuge, an escape from the grief she'd created for herself. And that's when she remembered him, that guy she used to know who was so kind and always seemed to know what to say. The sensitive man who always listened without judgment and with honest concern.

Unsure whether he'd even remember her given their long separation, she decided to call him. After all, what did she have to lose? She was a little surprised when he not only answered the phone but seemed excited to hear from her. Right away he told her he'd be delighted to see her, and they made plans to meet for coffee and catch up.

When he saw her, it was like no time had passed since the day they'd last seen each other. He still loved her with his whole heart and was certain he would love her forever.

The two talked for hours. The girl's side of the conversation was pretty superficial at first, but soon her emotions took over and she began to tell him about all the things that had gone wrong since they last saw each other. She told him about all her mistakes and how she'd been so wrong about so much. But, rather than telling her "I told you so" or anything like that, he just listened. And though one could hardly blame him if they had, his feelings about her didn't change as horrid details of the last few years spilled out across the table. Instead, the man's heart broke for this girl who had gone through so much.

The girl noticed something peculiar as they talked. Though the man across from her had not changed, the way she saw him did. His kindness and unconditional love began to melt her hardened heart. And as that happened, she stopped thinking of him as the "too nice" guy. Instead, she realized he was what she had been looking for all along. It wasn't charisma and big muscles that could fill her heart; pursuing such things had only left her cold. Instead, her heart was filled by the deep regard for her she found in this gentle man who made her feel whole. Once she finally got that, he finally got her. And the two are still together to this day.

The girl in the story is me. The man who wins her heart is Jesus. And yes, He remains the love of my life. (My husband, Bill, is a close second.)

I didn't have to change to come to Jesus. I didn't have to clean myself up or straighten my life out. I just had to approach Him in faith. Some people believe they are too bad or have messed up too much for Jesus to love them. I know there were times I thought that about myself. But like we discussed earlier in this chapter, God's love isn't dependent on who we are or on what we've done. He loved me just the way I was. He loves you just the way you are. And He loves us enough not to leave us that way. When received, His love changes us.

When we finally surrender to the relentless love of God presented to us through Jesus, He comes in and cleans us up. He changes our misguided desires to reflect His own righteous desires. He binds up our wounds. He mends our broken places. He fills us with His joy and peace and grace. There may still be consequences we have to face or difficult times to walk through because of our pasts, but we won't have to face anything alone.

God's love amazes me! The Creator of the cosmos loves me as a Father (2 Corinthians 6:18). And He sent

His Son Jesus to love me as my spiritual bridegroom
(Isaiah 62:5). And His Holy Spirit guides and comforts me,
loving me like a best friend would (John 14:16; 15:15).
The Lord's love is enough to fill every hole, every void,
every longing.

I want us to take one more look at 1 Corinthians
13:2-8. But this time I've changed the word "love" and the
pronouns referring to it to "God" in order that we might
really take to heart the way He relates to His sons and
daughters.

> *"[God] is patient, [God] is kind. [God]
> does not envy, [God] does not boast, [God]
> is not proud. [God] does not dishonor
> others, [God] is not self-seeking, [God] is
> not easily angered, [God] keeps no record
> of wrongs. [God] does not delight in evil
> but rejoices in the truth. [God] always
> protects, always trusts, always hopes,
> always perseveres. [God] never fails."* (1
> Corinthians 13:4-8, NIV)

Let's start reshaping our view of God by *believing*
the truth of His love for us. And, in our interactions with
others, let us seek to reflect it.

You, precious friend, are loved.

Questions for Group or Personal Reflection:

1. How does God's love for us differ from the way the world defines love?

2. Which characteristic of true love described in 1 Corinthians 13:4-8 is the easiest for you to show others? Which is the hardest?

3. In what ways have you settled for counterfeit love from others?

4. What is it that sometimes makes it hard for you to believe that God could love you unconditionally? What specific truth from this chapter might help to calm that fear?

Chapter 3

You Are Reborn

"If anyone is in Christ, he is a new creation.
The old has passed away; behold, the new has
come."

2 Corinthians 5:17

J ust as our parents are only our parents if we are born of them—either through natural birth or adoption—we must be born of God if we are to be His children. Our rebirth, which is sometimes referred to as being born again, is a fundamental aspect of the Christian faith. Because this spiritual rebirth is essential to new life in Christ, I would be doing you a great disservice if I did not spend some time explaining this pivotal aspect of our identities. Grasping this topic will help us claim everything else God has for us, His beloved daughters. So, here we go!

Context for the New Birth Concept

In John 3 we are introduced to a man named Nicodemus. He was a Pharisee, a Jewish scholar and teacher of the law. And one night while Jesus was in Jerusalem, Nicodemus decided to pay Him a visit. That Nicodemus approached under the cover of darkness is telling. Likely he would've preferred no one know about it.

Jesus had been performing miracles, of which the Pharisees didn't approve, and had even caused quite a ruckus at the temple. His actions were gaining some unfavorable attention from the religious leaders. Most Pharisees were very verbal in their opposition toward Jesus, so meeting with Him could have gotten Nicodemus in a bit of trouble with his peers. Nevertheless, there was something in him that decided talking to Jesus personally was worth the risk. There was something he just had to tell Him: "Rabbi, we know that you are a teacher come from God, for no one can do these signs that you do unless God is with him" (John 3:2).

In saying this Nicodemus was affirming his belief that Jesus was indeed a man sent with God's authority and purpose. That's a pretty big statement considering that most of the religious leaders at that time were trying to figure out how to discredit Jesus, not affirm Him. So for Nicodemus to announce that he believed Jesus was sent from God could have been considered a very radical move on his part.

But interestingly, instead of validating his courage, Jesus responded to Nicodemus with a bold declaration of His own: "Unless one is born again he cannot see the kingdom of God" (John 3:3).

Because of the way the rest of the conversation unfolded, I'm inclined to believe that Nicodemus was caught a little off guard by this response. I can just imagine him cocking his head to the side, his brow slightly furrowed, as he scratched his head and said, "Huh?" Surely things weren't going the way he'd anticipated.

But rather than taking offense at Jesus's seemingly elusive response—as most Pharisees who felt challenged by Jesus would do—Nicodemus continued to press Him for a clear answer. He sought understanding. It's pride that sets us up to be offended or disappointed when God doesn't answer the way we think He ought to, and Nicodemus's words here are a great cue for the rest of us. He asked, "How can a man be born again when he is old? Can he enter a second time into his mother's womb?" (John 3:4).

Nicodemus's confusion boiled down to misunderstanding. He was very educated in the Hebrew Scriptures and Jewish traditions. He'd likely performed all the ritual cleansings, or mikvahs, that were required for someone in his position and then some. And as a Pharisee Nicodemus would have also fulfilled the Pharisaical requirements for being "born again" (i.e. Bar mitzvah at the age of 13, being married, ordained as rabbi, and the head of a rabbinical school in Israel). He would have also been familiar with the custom for Gentiles who wished to convert to Judaism in which such persons were fully immersed in water as a symbolic washing away of their former pagan life as they emerged to a new life as covenant members of God's family. This tradition was known as their "new birth." But because biological Jews were already children of God through Abraham, and

Nicodemus was a Jew through and through, there was no need for him to be reborn in this way either.

A helpful side note here is that the Jewish people were expecting their Messiah, the Savior who had been foretold to them in Scripture, to come in like a great warrior to rescue them from the oppression of the Romans. Instead of anticipating a Messiah who would atone for their sins through His death, they were expecting the same type of deliverance God employed when He redeemed their ancestors out of Egypt and led them into the Promised Land. It was their belief that a powerful man like King David would charge in and subdue their enemies, ushering in a lasting reign of peace and prosperity for the restored kingdom of Israel. It would be under this Messiah's rule, they expected, that all the people of the world would become Jewish. What Jesus had really come to do was not even on their radar.

As Jesus went on to clarify that "unless one is born of water and the Spirit, he cannot enter the kingdom of God. That which is born of the flesh is flesh, and that which is born of the Spirit is spirit" (John 3:5-6), Jesus took everything Nicodemus thought he knew and flipped it upside down. His words implied that the new kingdom that was to be ushered in by the Messiah was not going to be one established in this world but in the hearts of men. It was not going to be set up using political influence but by the internal submission of one's heart to the lordship of Christ. God's kingdom was to be a spiritual kingdom that required a spiritual birth if one was to gain entrance into it. Simply being a descendant of Abraham wasn't enough.

The underlying point I want you to grasp here is that looking through the lens of human tradition alone was enough to make Nicodemus miss what Jesus was really saying, and it can do the same to us. Even extensive education in the Scriptures can't help us understand things only discerned by the Spirit. Consider this passage, one that was surely familiar to Nicodemus, which God spoke to Israel through the prophet Ezekiel:

> *"I will sprinkle clean water on you, and you will be clean; I will cleanse you from all your impurities and from all your idols. I will give you a new heart and put a new spirit in you; I will remove from you your heart of stone and give you a heart of flesh. And I will put my Spirit in you and move you to follow my decrees and be careful to keep my laws."* (Ezekiel 36:25-27, NIV)

This verse is a foreshadowing of what God would fulfill through the promised Messiah for all who believed. Nicodemus missed the spiritual significance of this Scripture (at least initially) because he wasn't looking at it with spiritual eyes.

In Galatians 3:26-29 Paul speaks of the fulfillment of this promise when he says,

> *"In Christ Jesus you are all sons of God, through faith. For as many of you as were baptized into Christ have put on Christ. There is neither Jew nor Greek, there is neither slave nor free, there is no male and female, for you are all one in Christ Jesus. And if you are Christ's, then you are Abraham's offspring, heirs according to promise."*

The clarification given here wasn't available to Nicodemus, whose encounter with Jesus occurred years before the Galatians passage was written. I point this out because having an extensive knowledge of biblical theology isn't what's going to save us. Christianity is not about knowledge; it's about relationship. There are times when God will reveal more spiritual wisdom to us in one intimate conversation with Him then we'll find in hours of trying to study the Bible on our own. I can't stress enough how important it is to seek the heart of our Abba Father above all else.

To his credit, Nicodemus didn't give up on getting a clear answer even when he couldn't quite connect the dots; instead, he kept asking for better understanding. And I believe that as a result of that, this was the night on which Nicodemus began his journey to rebirth. While on this evening Nicodemus approached Jesus in secret, he would eventually publicly defend Jesus to other Pharisees (John 7:45-52). And a day would come when he would help take Jesus's lifeless body from the cross and tenderly prepare it for burial (John 19:39-40). I'd say that speaks volumes to a change in his heart.

Inward Change, Outward Expression

The later events of Nicodemus's life are a beautiful reminder that spiritual rebirth is always accompanied by physical transformation. When we believe the truth about our Abba Father, it is evidenced in the way we think and in how we live. The inner change that goes on when God gives life to our hearts of stone begins to express itself outwardly. A sure sign of our salvation, in fact, is in the tangible shift in our attitudes and behaviors toward others that rises from our desire to please God.

Interestingly, the Bible often compares those who love and trust in God to trees. Indeed, the moment the seed of faith sprouts in a heart, a person is born again into God's kingdom. As that plant grows and takes over within an individual, he or she becomes an "[oak] of righteousness, the planting of the LORD, that he might be glorified" (Isaiah 61:3). New birth through trusting in Christ marks just the beginning of new life for a believer. After that, our new faith is supposed to grow, mature, and produce much fruit. It should be a major part of our lives.

I'm amazed that each little fruit tree seed contains all the things necessary for it to grow into a mature, thriving tree that will produce lots of fruit. The same could be said of the seed of faith planted in our hearts: it contains all we will need to grow in our maturity as daughters of God. But it's important to remember that seeds don't become fruit bearers overnight. First, baby trees have to sprout out of the ground as tiny saplings.

Think of a new Christian as an eager baby tree. At the earliest stage in the faith journey, a believer's roots are just starting to spread as her trunk and branches slowly gain strength. She is establishing the foundation necessary for the production of fruit in the future. Most fruit trees must wait several years before they are able to produce fruit; some can even take up to seven or eight years.[12] So if you're just getting started in the faith journey and feel like you're not producing much noticeable fruit yet, don't get discouraged. Remember that literal trees develop the necessary strength needed for the job ahead before they begin producing. And as they do, they must also work at the task of growing the leaves necessary for soaking up the sun's rays to support the crop to come. As Galatians 6:9 reminds us, "In due season, we will reap, if we do not give up."

Leaves are among the very first external characteristics that visually set apart one kind of tree from another. I have three types of fruit trees in my backyard: apple, lemon, and peach. And even when they don't have any fruit on their branches, I can still tell them apart from each other and from the other trees in my yard because of their leaves. In a similar way, our leaves, the characteristics inherent in a daughter of God, are one of the key ways that people can tell us apart from unbelievers. In the same way people are able to distinguish a biker from a businessman or a pizza delivery guy from a police officer, we should be distinguishable to the rest of the world as being the children of God—even if we're new to Christianity.

When I went to India on a mission trip years ago, each of us women were given a traditional Indian dress. A sari is a beautiful, long piece of fabric that is wrapped and folded, then wrapped and folded again, and draped in such a way that the one wearing it looks and feels like a princess. But putting one on is hard to do. The first time I wore one, in fact, I had to have one of the Indian locals that we were working with help me and my daughter put ours on right.

When we got back to the U.S., I was excited to wear mine to church to show it off to my friends. But I failed miserably at the task of putting it on and had to go back and watch some videos on the Internet and practice several times before I could wear it in a way that even closely resembled how it was supposed to look.

When we are new Christians, we're only just learning how to stop making provisions for our flesh and to put on Christ (Romans 13:14). And at first, that can feel as tricky as trying to drape a sari without a tutorial. Nevertheless, Colossians 2:12 and 14 tell us to clothe ourselves with "compassionate hearts, kindness, humility, meekness, and patience. And above all these put on love, which binds everything together in perfect harmony." We won't get that right every time. In fact, it takes a lot of practice and patience to do it well. Even for longtime Christians, exemplifying such things can be hard to do. But with God's help, we can. And we must try.

Learning to love our enemies, to forgive offenders, and to live sacrificially are not normal human inclinations. We have to develop new habits and thought patterns that are contrary to our flesh and former way of life. Depending on where we started from, what our lives looked like before our new births, this process may be harder for some than for others. I, for instance, was one who needed a lot of work. But I can tell you from experience that God is willing to walk alongside us and doesn't expect perfection. None of us will achieve perfection this side of heaven. But what we should be aiming for each day is a marked pattern of growth, a visual transformation from the image of our old selves into the image of Christ. And we can find instruction on how to grow by interacting with God's Word each day and asking Him to help us apply what we learn.

Over time a sapling matures into a young tree, gaining girth and height. And as I think about the maturation of the Christian, Psalm 1:3 comes to mind. It says "He [who delights in the Lord] is like a tree planted by streams of water that yields its fruit in its season, and its leaf does not wither." This reminds me that the characteristics of a child of God grow more obvious as we plant ourselves ever more deeply in the Lord. It also reminds me that as a maturing believer, I really am to bear fruit for God's glory.

Purposes of Fruit Bearing

Allow me to pause here for a moment to clarify that salvation is not earned by works; we have been saved by grace alone. It is a free gift from a benevolent God to entirely unworthy creatures. But what I want to drive home as we begin discussing the topic of fruit bearing is that our faith is *proven* by the works it produces. As the apostle James said,

> *"Unless it produces good deeds, [faith] is dead and useless. Now someone may argue, 'Some people have faith, others have good deeds.' But I say, 'How can you show me your faith if you don't have good deeds? I will show you my faith by my good deeds.' ... Can't you see that faith without good deeds is useless?"* (James 2:17-18, 20, NLT)

The works James talks about here aren't deeds done to show commitment to the law—as if that could earn God's favor. He's talking about holiness, about choosing to do good things out of a desire to please God and to thank Him for the salvation He's given. Our works are the good fruit produced through our lives in accordance to our faith.

All believers must take seriously the call to bear good fruit. God's will is that, as we grow in our wisdom and understanding of who He is and who He created us to be, we walk in a way that honors Him. He wants our lives to produce good works of every kind (Colossians 1:10). The New Testament has over thirty passages referring to bearing fruit according to the Spirit, and there are three main purposes for doing so.

First, the fruit we produce is meant to meet the needs of others. A tree's fruit does not benefit the tree itself; instead, it blesses those who come in contact with it. Fruit is a source of nourishment. Jesus told us that "even the Son of Man came not to be served but to serve, and to give his life as a ransom for many" (Mark 10:45). We express fruit when we use the resources we have to serve the needs of those around us, to nourish and sustain them.

The faith thriving within us is what persuades us to love our neighbors, to feed the hungry, to minister to the sick and broken hearted. It stirs compassion so that we aren't content to simply acknowledge a need but are compelled to do something about it. Of course, we won't physically be able to meet every need we come across. And not every need can be adequately met by every Christian. We all receive different gifts and abilities. And we are given unique ministries and callings. But if nothing else, we can stand in fervent prayer with our brothers and sisters and strive to meet the needs God enables us to meet with the strength He provides.

The second purpose of fruit production is to invite others to "taste and see that the LORD is good" (Psalm 34:8). It is through our fruit that we help others come to know the goodness of our Heavenly Father. We are His hands and feet. It is through the church, through each of us, that the world can experience God's all-satisfying love and grace. When we use our fruit to point to the One who is the source of our fruit, they get a taste of God's goodness for themselves.

The third purpose of bearing fruit is reproduction. Fruit, after all, contains the seeds that have the potential to become more trees. In Genesis 1:28 God told Adam and Eve to "be fruitful and multiply." This was the same message He gave to Noah's family as they stepped off the ark (Genesis 9:1). Throughout the book of Acts, as the church was getting its start, "the word of God increased and multiplied" (Acts 12:24), and the believers "increased in number daily" (Acts 16:5).

In 2 Corinthians Paul tells us that "God gives seed to farmers and provides everyone with food. He will increase what you have, so that you can give even more to those in need" (2 Corinthians 9:10, CEV). He goes on to say that this is "much more than a service that supplies God's people with what they need. It is something that will make many others thank God" (2 Corinthians 9:13, CEV). The ultimate purpose of the fruit we produce is to bring others to an awareness of God's saving grace. To bring them the seed, faith in the Word of God, that can grow in their hearts so they too can become oaks of

77

righteousness for the Lord.

Romans 10:17 says that "faith comes from hearing, and hearing through the word of Christ." Telling people about Jesus, sharing the good news of the gospel, sharing about the hope we have been given as children of God, and inviting others to experience the same is how we help plant seeds for the kingdom. We can do this in our homes, in our schools, in our neighborhoods, in our jobs, and even to the ends of the earth.

The Purpose of Maturation

Of course the day comes when a young tree is considered a mature tree. It resembles the one described in Jeremiah 17:7-8:

> *"Blessed is the man who trusts in the LORD,*
> *whose trust is the LORD.*
> *He is like a tree planted by water,*
> *that sends out its roots by the stream,*
> *and does not fear when heat comes,*
> *for its leaves remain green,*
> *and is not anxious in the year of drought,*
> *for it does not cease to bear fruit."*

Believers at this stage in their lives have grown in their knowledge of, experience with, and confidence in our Heavenly Father. Their leaves, the distinguishing characteristics of a child of God, are more apparent and fruit producing is no longer seasonal but has now become a consistent part of their lives. And as mature trees, they have weathered many storms throughout their lives—some small, some fierce, but all of them used by God for the believers' good.

As I think about this, I'm reminded of a time a few years ago when my husband had to do some work in Tucson, Arizona. While he was there, my son and I had the chance to visit him for a week. There were plenty of fun and beautiful places to explore in that part of the country, and I remember that one spot we visited was called Biosphere II.

Biosphere II is a massive facility that was built in the eighties as a sort of social/scientific experiment. Inside this facility made mostly of glass and large steel support beams, are areas created to represent different climate zones from around the world. For instance, there was a tropical rainforest zone, a desert zone, and a grassland zone, among others. There was also an area designed for farming and a living quarters where they had planned to house a select group of people. These selected individuals were to live inside the facility for a full year with little to no contact with the outside world. They could only eat food grown in the facility, and they could only treat minor illnesses and injuries with what they had inside.

When the experiment began, there were doctors and scientists who worked in the buildings that surrounded Biosphere II. They monitored the health and well-being of the people living inside it. They wanted to keep track of their struggles, successes, and how well they were able to adapt and survive in that type of environment. In spite of their oversight and interest, however, the experiment turned out to be a big failure. Not one single person was able to live out the entire year within Biosphere II.

As our tour guide led us through the buildings, explaining the campus history and its purpose as well as the ways they still make use of the facility today, we noticed something strange. Many of the large branches on the trees inside Biosphere II were tied to the support beams overhead.

When we asked our guide if there was a reason for this, he explained that the trees in the facility were fairly weak and brittle. The ropes were necessary because the trees were not strong enough to support their own large branches. Should the branches break off, they could cause severe damage. This situation, he went on to explain, was a result of there being no wind or storms inside the Biosphere. The rocking and bending that trees experience as a result of wind and storms is what helps them develop strength and flexibility. Because these particular trees had never experienced the necessary strain needed to develop those things because they had only existed inside the shelter of Biosphere II, they had never reached their full potential.

At this news, my very wise husband looked at me and said, "That's why God allows the storms in our lives too." Bad things will happen to us. Hard times are going to come. But when we face them under the watchful eye of our Abba Father, He will use them to help us come out stronger and more resilient. A mature believer has faced strong winds and weathered fierce storms and found that God is indeed worthy of trust. The more difficulties we face, then, the more opportunities we have to see the provision of God's sovereignty in our lives. Our relationship with God is what will sustain us in the storms, the droughts, the scorching heat, and the bitter cold.

There are times I like to think of myself as a mature Christian. Like I have somehow arrived. It's kind of like that moment as an adult when you first felt like an adult instead of just a kid trying to act like a grown-up. But in truth, there are also days when I feel like I've regressed to a little sapling again: I feel spiritually weak, small, and fragile. And in these times, I wonder if I will ever reach the stage of maturity that I see in the leaders I look up to.

In fact, I experienced a time like this recently.

Rather than feeling like a confident, strong, and well-rooted tree, I was feeling pretty puny and fruitless. But it was in that season that God began to teach me about a stage all cultivated fruit trees must go through: pruning.

Every year, usually in the late winter, I cut back many of the trees and shrubs in my yard. After they have been trimmed, they can look pretty scraggly. Most of their leaves are gone, their branches are thinned, and there is no fruit to speak of. But, as their gardener, I know that pruning is actually for their benefit.

Pruning serves several purposes. First, it removes any dead or diseased branches. If left intact, such branches could negatively impact the health of the entire plant. Removing them helps prevent insects and harmful organisms from entering the tree and causing decay.

Dead or diseased branches in the life of a believer are things like sin, compromised convictions, disobedience, fear, idols, and false beliefs that have been embraced as truth. Such things will keep us from producing fruit in accordance with God's kingdom initiative. In John 15:1-2, Jesus tells us that God is our gardener and that He prunes away any branch that is not bearing fruit. He doesn't want them to have an imperiling effect on the other branches or on our lives as a whole.

An experienced gardener knows that not only does he need to prune the sick and dead branches away, but he also must trim back the healthy ones. Trimming the good branches benefits a tree in several ways. One, it allows the tree to take a break. Trees need to rest from fruit production from time to time so they can expand their root systems, which in turn strengthens their foundation and enables the roots to reach deeper into its source of nourishment. Two, when a healthy branch is pruned properly, two or three new branches will grow back in its place, thereby increasing the tree's potential yield.

This type of pruning can often be the hardest to understand when you experience it. You may wonder why something that seemed to be flourishing, something good and fruitful in your life, has just been cut off. But you are wise to remember that Jesus tells us that not only does God remove the fruitless branches, but "every branch that does bear fruit he prunes, so that it may bear more" (John 15:2).

As I close out this discussion about rebirth into God's family and the accompanying maturation process, I want to point out John 15:4. Jesus said that "as the branch cannot bear fruit by itself, unless it abides in the vine, neither can you, unless you abide in me." Indeed, staying connected to our source of life is crucial for us becoming trees of righteousness for the Lord. If we are not intentional in remaining in Christ, the storms of life will uproot us, the trials of life will wither us, and the pleasures of this world will draw our roots away from the living water that is the Word of God and will submerge us in the polluted waters of the desires of the flesh.

You and I have been reborn not so we can walk around calling ourselves Christians and think that's enough but so that we can live a new life. A life full of good- fruit-bearing. The apostle Peter ends his second letter with a charge for believers to "grow in the grace and knowledge of our Lord and Savior Jesus Christ" (2 Peter 3:18). And that is what we must do. It is the grace and knowledge of God's Word that gives us the nourishment that will cause us to grow into mature, fruit-bearing trees for God's glory.

If you and I were to step back and examine the fruit produced in our lives, what would it look like? Would it reflect the fruit of the Spirit, which is love, joy, peace, patience, kindness, goodness, faithfulness, gentleness, and self-control (Galatians 5:22-23)? Would such things be evident in our attitudes? Or are our lives more characteristic of the works of the flesh—producing things like sexual sin, impurity, sensuality, idolatry, strife, jealousy, and fits of anger (Galatians 5:19-21)?

Frankly, bits from both of those lists may show up in us, no matter how mature in our faith we have become.

But it helps to remember that as long as we live this side of heaven, our flesh and our spirit will be at war with each other (1 Peter 2:11). Living according to the Spirit of God, then, is a choice we must make daily. Paul therefore urges us to be quick to throw off our old sinful nature and to put on the new nature we receive through our new birth, the nature created in the image of God our Father (Ephesians 4:22-24). As we continue to do this and to mature in our faith, the works of the flesh will decrease and the fruit of the Spirit will increase; thus, every day, little by little, we will look more like Christ.

Living a good Christian life, bearing fruit in obedience to God, isn't about being perfect. It's about living a life that is sold out to Jesus. It's about really truly wanting to look more like Him every day and intentionally allowing the faith within your heart to flourish and to bear the fruit of righteousness. Being born again is so much more than a one-time decision to follow Jesus. Rebirth is just the beginning of a whole new life.

Questions for Group and Personal Reflection

1. What insight from the story of Nicodemus most resonated with you?

2. Consider the stages of growth for trees. With what stage of growth do you best identify as you think about your Christian walk today?

3. What evidence of good fruit bearing can be seen in your life?

4. What are some ways you can intentionally stay connected to your source of nourishment so that you continue to grow in the grace and knowledge of Christ?

Chapter 4

You Are Forgiven

"If we confess our sins,

he is faithful and just to forgive us our sins and to

cleanse us from all unrighteousness."

1 John 1:9

N ext to the rebirth concept covered in the previous chapter, our understanding of the forgiveness we receive as children of God has the greatest potential for impacting every aspect of our spiritual growth. After all, not feeling like we have been forgiven can cause us to feel ashamed, unloved, guilty, and defeated. And harboring feelings of unforgiveness toward others can lead to things like pride, bitterness, hostility, and resentment. When applied, however, forgiveness is the ointment that can heal wounds, restore brokenness, and soothe aching hearts. And it's available to us simply because we are God's children.

Let's begin by making sure we grasp what God's forgiveness entails.

First, we need to understand the depravity of our sin, the seriousness of our situation before we placed faith in Christ. In the intro to his book, *Made for His Pleasure*, Alistair Begg writes, "Only when we acknowledge the gravity of our condition—that we are suffering from a terminal illness the Bible calls 'sin'—will we understand our need for a Savior. We will never come to know the Lord Jesus Christ as a reality until we see Him as a necessity."[13]

Sadly, as a whole, professing Christians have fallen into a pattern of rating personal sins on a scale. We say things like, "What she did was way worse than what I did," or "At least I'm not as bad as that guy!" We fail to remember that the penalty for our supposed lesser sins is just as severe as it is for those we like to think of as being worse. This suggests we have lost a sense of our deep need for the Savior who came to cleanse us from *all* our sins.

The Bible tells us that "whoever keeps the whole law but fails in one point has become guilty of all of it" (James 2:10). This means that the one who stole bubble gum from the store is just as guilty before God as the one who murdered someone. The person who dishonored her parents is just as guilty as the one who cheated on her husband. We have all sinned and fallen woefully short of God's standard (Romans 3:23), which is His own holiness, and the reality is that none of us deserve His forgiveness. In fact, our situation was so desperate that nothing but faith in Jesus Christ and His atoning sacrifice on our behalf could acquit us of our sins and make us right with God. Only His blood is precious enough to pay off the debt for our sins. Only His death can take the place of ours (Galatians 1:4). God took the certificate of debt that was against each of us and nailed it to the cross of Christ (Colossians 2:14).

If we are to really live in light of God's wonderful gift of forgiveness, we've got to accept that all sin grieves the heart of our Abba Father. We've got to trust that He encourages believers to turn their backs on sin not simply because He said so, but because He knows the devastating effects sin will ultimately have on our lives.

Perhaps an illustration will help here. I've got several food allergies. Thankfully none of them are life threatening, but the reactions that certain foods cause me are enough to keep me from wanting to eat those things. As much as I would love to consume pizza or Indian food, I've learned that the momentary enjoyment of doing so isn't worth the price I'll have to pay later. Not only would I have to suffer through the initial reaction of eating something off limits, but my strained immune system would then cause inflammation that could lead to long-term damage to my body. The negative consequences are not only immediate but can cause future damage.

We as Christians must remember that although sinning may seem good at the time—as satisfying as that initial taste of pizza would be for me—the effects it can have on our spiritual, emotional, and even physical selves are far reaching. Much greater than you or I can even imagine. We've got to know that indulging in it exacts a cost. And worse, it makes light of what Jesus did on our behalf.

Forgiveness is the fullness of God's great mercy toward those who believe (Ephesians 2:4-5). And if we really get what a fantastic gift it is, we will strive to stay as far from sinning as we can. So, let's take a closer look at what forgiveness means for us.

Although I could write an entire book on this topic, we're going to look at only three specifics facets of forgiveness in this chapter. The first is accepting Christ's forgiveness for our pasts, the second is applying Christ's forgiveness to our present, and the third is extending Christ's forgiveness to others.

Accepting Christ's Forgiveness for Our Pasts

Like many, I've made too many mistakes to count. Some sins seemed big, some seemed small, and some came with consequences I'll have to carry for the rest of my life. Thankfully, some of my mistakes have only affected me; others, however, have left scars on those that I love and cherish the most. Learning to separate myself from my own sins has proven difficult to say the least.

Perhaps part of the problem is that I tend to be a bit of a perfectionist. When I feel like I've fallen short of what was expected, let someone down, or just plain made a mess of things, I can be pretty hard on myself. But I think a bigger reason that I find it so difficult to accept that I am forgiven is because we have an adversary who loves to condemn us, reminding us of our mistakes incessantly and often. In fact, thoughts like, *How could you have done that?* or *You should have known better*, or *You're never going to live that one down*, are all enemy attempts to keep us from finding the freedom that comes from forgiveness. They do not reflect the heart behind God's decision to send His Son to die on the cross for us: Jesus came to set us free (Acts 10:43).

Scripture calls Satan the accuser (Revelation 12:10) and the father of lies (John 8:44). He wants to fill our minds with thoughts of self condemnation. In Christ, our sin-debt has been removed and we have been made new. If, however, Satan can make us continue to believe we are unable to overcome our mistakes, he can impede our ability to fulfill our God given purpose. Believing Satan's lies does not diminish the truth of God's Word, but it can hinder the freedom God's truth brings to our lives.

In Isaiah 43:25 we are told that God will blot out our sin and remember it no more. That He will "remember it no more" does not imply that God will forget our sin as if it simply slipped His mind; rather, it means that He will remove it from us. He will no longer bring to mind or hold us responsible for the sins for which we have been forgiven. Psalm 103:12-13 explains it this way: "As far as the east is from the west, so far does he remove our transgressions from us. As a father shows compassion to his children, so the LORD shows compassion to those who fear him."

Gossip, murderous thoughts, gluttony, adultery, lying, stealing, homosexual indulgence, pride, promiscuity, idols, rebellion: they are all sin. They all separate us from God. But they don't have the last word in our lives. Jesus does. And although we may not always be free from the physical consequences of our sin, our place in heaven with our Heavenly Father is secure. Once we accept Christ as Lord, we are separated from the very things that separated us from God in the first place.

Luke shares a story about a woman who experienced firsthand the freeing power of the Word of God toward those who dare to believe. What's recorded in Luke 7 tells about a certain night when Jesus was having dinner at a Pharisee's home and this woman came to see Him. Luke refers to her as "a woman of the city, who was a sinner" (Luke 7:37). The Bible doesn't say what her sins were, but it does tell us that they were "many" (Luke 7:47). I don't know about you, but that is a statement that could have very well been said about me—and I'm not sure that's how I would like to be remembered. (At least not unless it were attached to the rest of this woman's story.)

Although she was known as a "sinner," I think this visitor had finally reached the rock bottom of her personal sin pit some time before she visited Jesus. Let me explain what I mean by that. I'm talking about that place where a person has sunk to depths she never knew possible and can't bear to sink any lower but doesn't know how to climb her way out either. It's a place where I have certainly been, and "hopeless" doesn't even begin to describe what it feels like down there.

Sometimes I imagine what it was like for this woman when she first started to hear stories about a man named Jesus, a man who was healing people and forgiving their sins. Likely when she found out He was coming to her town and would be having dinner at a local Pharisee's house, hope began to creep up inside her broken soul. Whatever the case, it appears that she had to find out whether the stories were true. And she wanted to see if she too could find healing and forgiveness.

Luke records that this woman didn't say a word as she knelt down by Jesus's side; instead, she just began to weep, right there in front of everyone. And as she did, she began to wash His feet with her tears and dry them with her hair. She kissed Jesus's feet and anointed them with a bottle of very costly oil (Luke 7:38). Even knowing she was unworthy of mercy, she approached Him. With every bit of courage she could muster, she poured out her deep reverence for the Savior and acknowledged her desperate need for grace. These were the actions of a woman so broken and burdened that she was willing to risk the ridicule of the Pharisees just for a chance to find forgiveness.

I don't want you to miss the enormity of Jesus's two simple statements to this woman who threw herself on His mercy. The first words He spoke to her were these: "Your sins are forgiven" (Luke 7:48). Then two verses later, He said, "Your faith has saved you; go in peace" (Luke 7:49). And in accepting the truth of those words, she found that Jesus had changed the trajectory of her life forever. She was forgiven. She was set free. Jesus had removed from her the weight of her many sins and she left the house that night in peace.

Before we came to Christ, we were enemies of God—and there is no peace between God and His enemies. But now, as forgiven children, we receive a peace far beyond anything the world can offer. In fact, Jesus said to His disciples, "My peace I give to you. Not as the world gives do I give to you. Let not your hearts be troubled, neither let them be afraid" (John 14:27). And Paul reassured the church in Rome of this promise when he reminded them that "since we have been justified by faith, we have peace with God through our Lord Jesus Christ" (Romans 5:1).

Jesus has the last word when it comes to a believer's personal sin because He became the substitutionary sacrifice for our sins. He reconciled us by His physical body through His death on the cross so He could present us to God as holy in His sight, without blemish, and free from accusation (Colossians 1:22). As Romans 6:23 says, "The wages of sin is death, but the free gift of God is eternal life in Christ Jesus our Lord." So, if you sometimes think you have done too many things wrong and can't possibly be separated from your sins as thoroughly as the Bible says, think again. There is nothing too big or so bad that the blood of Christ cannot cover it. If you've placed your trust in Him, you are free.

Forgiveness of sin requires two things: sacrifice and repentance. Nothing short of sincere repentance accompanied by an equivalent sacrifice will achieve restoration between sinful man and holy God. Because of Christ's willingness to lay down His life in place of ours, we no longer have to bring sacrifices to an altar to find forgiveness. All we need to bring, as the woman did when she came to see Jesus that night, is a repentant heart (Luke 5:32; 2 Corinthians 7:10).

When the enemy whispers his lies to me, it helps to remember that the Bible never refers to believers as sinners but as saints. You, then, are a saint! And you don't have to perform some great feat of faith or wait until a religious leader says you've earned it to be able to claim your title. Instead, you and I have received this designation just because we are God's children. We have been saved by grace, forgiven our trespasses. We no longer have to wear that word "sinner" as if it's part of our identity (Ephesians 2:4-6; 1 Corinthians 1:2).

The *New Living Translation* uses the phrase "holy people" for the same word that is translated as "saints" in other Bible translations. Here's what 2 Thessalonians 1:10 says: "When [Jesus] comes on that day, he will receive glory from his *holy people*—praise from all who believe. *And this includes you*, for you believed" (emphasis added).

As a child of God you, my sweet sister, are a saint, reconciled to Him through the blood of Christ. You are no longer liable for the eternal penalty of your sin. Your slate has been wiped clean. And if God does not hold your past against you, you shouldn't hold it against yourself either.

The accuser says we are guilty. Our Redeemer says "there is no condemnation" for those in Christ (Romans 8:1). The accuser says we are damaged goods. Our Redeemer says the old things "have passed away," and we have been made "new" (2 Corinthians 5:17). No matter what you've done in the past, then, it does not change who you are now in Jesus (Galatians 6:14-16).

If you're carrying around guilt, regret, or shame, it's time to let it go. Lay it all down at the foot of the cross. Christ wants to fill you with His peace.

Applying Christ's Forgiveness to Our Present

Another blessing of being a child of God is that we don't have to be afraid of messing up. I don't mean that we don't need to remain on guard against sin. I mean that we don't have to fear that our salvation can be lost. Just because we are now children of God does not mean we are never going to falter in our walk with Him. We're still going to get it wrong from time to time no matter how hard we try to get it right. (Believe me, I know! And so does our Heavenly Father.) But in Romans we find Paul's assertion that "where sin increased, grace abounded all the more, so that, as sin reigned in death, grace also might reign through righteousness leading to eternal life through Jesus Christ" (Romans 5:20-21).

As he moves into chapter six of his letter to the Christians in Rome, Paul poses a very important question: "Are we to continue in sin that grace may abound?" (Romans 6:1). He goes on to answer with an unequivocal "No!" The purpose of our rebirth, and of the grace-drenched forgiveness we receive as God's children, is that we will walk not according to our old sinful nature but "in newness of life" (Romans 6:2, 4). Our old sinful selves were crucified with Christ so that we would no longer be slaves to sin (Romans 6:6).

The distinction between the life of a sinner and that of a saint, between an unbeliever and a child of God, is that sin no longer has control over God's daughters or sons. It's no longer in charge in our hearts. We have been set free from the power of sin through the power of the Holy Spirit. Paul underscores this point by reminding us that "sin will have no dominion over [us], since [we] are not under the law but under grace" (Romans 6:14). Paul then rephrases his initial question: "Are we to sin because we are not under the law but under grace? By no means!" (Romans 6:15).

I want to camp out on the word "grace" for a minute because it is the pivot upon which our faith rests. It was out of his own desire to see that the Christians in Rome understood the meaning of grace that Paul emphasized this point so strongly in his letter.

The biblical definition of grace is the unmerited favor and kindness of God toward totally unworthy human beings. The *Zondervan Illustrated Bible Dictionary* explains it this way: "Grace is not merely the initiatory act of God that secures the believers' eternal salvation, but also that which maintains it throughout all of the Christian's life."[14] Indeed, it is through grace that we find the power to persevere in our new lives as His children (Acts 20:32).

Paul knew that the struggle between the sinful flesh and the born again spirit within the believer is strong. In fact, he said, "I have the desire to do what is right, but not the ability to carry it out" (Romans 7:18). This was his way of admitting his own frustrations of being set free from sin on the one hand, yet still having to live in a fallen world where Satan actively seeks to exert what limited power and authority he has, constantly tempting us to give in to the desires of this world. Paul knew—and oh my goodness, don't I know it too—that if we rely on our flesh being willing to live out a life of holiness, we will never be able to live above the pull of our lingering sinful desires. And that's what is so wonderful about having the grace of God available to us each day.

First Corinthians 10:13 says, "No temptation has come upon you except what is common to humanity. But God is faithful; He will not allow you to be tempted beyond what you are able, but with the temptation he will also provide a way out so that you may be able to bear it" (CSB).

What this tells us is that the way we apply Christ's forgiveness to our present is by drawing on the power of God's grace that is available to us as His children. Doing so allows us to put to death the sinful desires of the flesh and live for righteousness. God can and will help us overcome the sin in our lives. So let's heed the advice of Galatians 5:1, which states, "For freedom Christ has set us free; stand firm therefore, and do not submit again to a yoke of slavery." God wants us to be free from the bondage of our addictions, our struggles, our selfish desires.

Frankly, I have to draw on the strength of God's grace on a daily basis. My flesh is weak, and Satan knows the exact spots where it is the weakest. There are times when his attacks are fierce, and it is only by God's grace that I don't lose the battle. Even so, there are times when I forget that God's grace is bigger than my struggle and I give in to whatever temptation the enemy offers. I falter. Sometimes I fall flat on my face. But, even when I do, I know God's grace is there to help me back up and give me the courage to try again.

As Paul made clear, grace does not give us license to make a habit of sinning. But if we do sin, we don't have to walk around afraid that the wrath of God will fall on us. As God's children, after all, we have not received a spirit that makes us fearful; rather, we have received God's own Spirit by which we can cry out, "Abba! Father!" (Romans 8:15). Our Heavenly Father didn't sacrifice so much on our behalf just so He could brush us off the first time we messed things up (or the second time, or third, or one-hundred-forty-seventh). God's forgiveness isn't a one-time gift; it is a continual outpouring of His grace as many times and as often as we need it.

Dietrich Bonhoeffer, a German pastor-turned-spy during WWII, lived out his faith so completely that he risked everything to oppose the evil around him. Bonhoeffer was eventually killed in a Nazi concentration camp for his unwavering love and devotion to God's truth. Bonhoeffer lived out the forgiveness and grace he had been given, wholly devoted to sharing that truth with others.

When trying to sum up such a remarkable life of faith, biographer Eric Metaxas wrote, "Being a Christian is less about cautiously avoiding sin than about courageously and actively doing God's will."[15] I think this captures what the psalmist wrote: "But with you [God], there is forgiveness, so that we can, with reverence, serve you" (Psalm 130:4 NIV). You see, this is the point of God's forgiveness as applied to our present. The Lord wants us to serve Him by the power of His Holy Spirit in us, without fear and in perfect peace. Trusting in His grace to cover our sin gives us courage and boldness and confidence to live each day in service to Him. And when we are actively and courageously doing God's will, we by default are avoiding sin.

I love what Paul said in Hebrews 12:1-2: "Let us strip off every weight that slows us down, especially the sin that so easily trips us up. And let us run with endurance the race God has set before us. We do this by keeping our eyes on Jesus, the champion who initiates and perfects our faith" (NLT). Indeed, let us actively rely on the grace we have been given so we can live and serve in freedom.

Extending Christ's Forgiveness to Others

As we close this chapter, I want to discuss one more way that the forgiveness of God can revolutionize our present experiences. The restoration we receive as forgiven daughters of our Heavenly Father isn't meant to end with us. It should also impact our relationships with others.

I think the best place to start here is in admitting that there are times when we need people to forgive us— a humbling fact that should make it easier to extend grace as necessary. Seeking forgiveness can be as simple as saying, "I was wrong to speak to you that way. I'm so sorry. Will you please forgive me?" But in other instances, particularly if you've allowed time to pass or the offense was more serious, there might be need for a confrontation. True, there may be emotions you don't want to acknowledge or consequences you don't want to face that would hold you back from making things right and you may not receive the forgiveness you are seeking; nevertheless, we as God's daughters have an obligation to pursue peace (1 Peter 3:9-11).

An important part of seeking forgiveness is making restitution whenever it is necessary and possible. For instance, if I knocked down my neighbor's mailbox as I backed out of my driveway one morning, saying "I'm sorry" wouldn't be enough. In that case I would need to pay for the repairs to their mailbox as well as for any other damages I caused.

Of course, there will be times when restitution won't be as easy as replacing someone's mailbox. We may not be able to repair the damage we've done, fix what was broken, or restore what was lost. There will also be times when, given our best attempt, the person from whom we are seeking forgiveness will prove unwilling to give it. In such cases, it is helpful to remember that we are not culpable for another's response. Once we've done our part, we can only pray that our attempt at making amends will serve as seeds that will eventually sprout and allow them to forgive and heal.

Restoration may not always be possible, but we need to make every effort to pursue that goal anyway. Doing so is so important to God that Jesus tells us it should come even before our worship. Look at what He said in

Matthew 5:23-24: "If you are about to place your gift on the altar and remember that someone is angry with you, leave your gift there in front of the altar. Make peace with that person then come back and offer your gift" (CEV).

Given what God has done for us through Christ, our lives as Christians should be characterized by an attitude of repentance. Let me be clear that this doesn't mean we need to walk around feeling guilty all the time. But we do need to have an acute awareness of sin and a determination not to allow sin to rule in our lives, remaining quick to admit our wrongs and to heal damages we've caused.

Now it's time to talk about extending forgiveness to those who have hurt us. (I know, I know. Sometimes that's easier said than done, especially when the wounds are deep.) But when Jesus taught His disciples to pray, He included within the model prayer the insight that God will forgive us for our sins but expects us to forgive others for theirs too (Matthew 6:12). We as God's children, after all, are no more deserving of forgiveness than anyone else. And because God showed us such great mercy, we are called—no, we are commanded—to show others the same.

Forgiving, though, is not something that comes naturally. It isn't a trait that is innate within our DNA. In fact, these days it seems many people are almost eager to take offense and even more determined to get even or hold a grudge. And sadly, this attitude isn't limited to non-believers. Even many in the church are plagued with bitterness and animosity toward others for things as small as which football team they choose to root for. The malice that saturates our social media, news outlets, and even the entertainment industry is astonishing. That we are so divided speaks volumes about the heart condition of our culture.

I point this out because on this fallen planet, we will inevitably suffer the consequences for other people's sin. But as Christian author and teacher Neil Anderson says, we can do so either in the "bondage of bitterness or the freedom of forgiveness."[16]

Maybe today you are struggling with deeply rooted pain that goes all the way back to elementary school when a few mean kids bullied you. Maybe your parents neglected you. Maybe your husband hurt you. Maybe you endured something much, much worse. I won't pretend to know exactly what burden you are carrying. Your scars no doubt look very different than my own. But please let me encourage you: we serve a Savior who knows our pain well. He knows exactly how you feel.

In securing our way to salvation, Christ suffered in both body and soul. In His soul He experienced rejection, persecution, and betrayal. In His body He experienced hunger, discomfort, and abuse to the point of death. Jesus was sold for thirty pieces of silver by one of His closest friends, handed over to be beaten, tried, and convicted of a crime He didn't commit. He was sentenced to a humiliating, excruciating, torturous death. Yes, He *knew* what it meant to suffer the consequences for another person's sin. And yet, His dying cry from the cross was a plea that God would forgive the very ones who'd put Him there (Luke 23:34).

Think about that for a minute. While the crowds were cheering on His suffering, the sinless Son of God was pleading for their acquittal. I used to wonder how Jesus could do that. How could He, having loved so well and been treated so badly, still want God to show them mercy? The answer, of course, is that He is divine.

Although we are called to be like Christ, we are not Him. Our spirits need lots of help to overcome our flesh. I believe Jesus modeled a shocking degree of compassion on His tormenters in part to remind us that while there are some sins we will never be able to forgive in our own strength, we can do it through the strength of the divine Holy Spirit within us. When Paul said he could "do all things through Christ" who strengthened him (Philippians 4:13), that included forgiving what felt unforgivable.

I have walked circles around my kitchen table, crying out to God and asking Him to help me not sin in my anger over the pain someone caused me. I have had people and circumstances pop into my mind years after an incident and felt the full weight of the resentment and pain they caused – that I thought I had fully let go – come rushing back as if it happened yesterday. And I know what it's like not to want to forgive but to wish you could see a person suffer the same way you have. But I can tell you that the Lord does help us to forgive if we'll ask.

God already knows our hearts, so we don't need to pretend we are ok or that we have let go or forgotten how we have been hurt. And we don't have to be afraid to tell Him when we feel hatred toward our enemies, that we want them to suffer, or even that we wish they were dead. After all, the Psalms are filled with cries from David, a man after God's own heart, who pleaded for vengeance against his enemies. So when you feel overwhelmed by the hurt of betrayal or the sting of offense, go to God with those emotions. It is in coming before His throne that we will find the grace and mercy we need to let go (Hebrews 4:16). It is where we will find strength, peace, healing, and freedom.

There is a line from the *Hunger Games: Catching Fire* that I believe speaks as a good reminder for us in times when we are struggling with extending forgiveness.

Near the end of the movie, Katniss lies crouching in the arena. She's confused and battle weary as the lines between good and evil, right and wrong, friend and foe have become increasingly blurred. But as she wrestles with how and whom she is supposed to fight, Finnick appeals to her to "remember who the real enemy is."

Paul reminds us that "we do not wrestle against flesh and blood, but ... against the spiritual forces of evil" (Ephesians 6:12). Those we perceive as our enemies, then, the ones who've hurt us or wronged us or betrayed us, are not really our enemies. They are just pawns in a much bigger battle in which the ultimate enemy of our souls seeks to bog us down with bitterness and to keep us from reflecting the love and grace Christ offers.

How frustrated the devil must be when we refuse to hang onto hurt and instead live out the truth of Romans 12:19-21:

> *"Beloved, never avenge yourselves, but leave it to the wrath of God, for it is written, 'Vengeance is mine, I will repay, says the Lord.' To the contrary, 'if your enemy is hungry, feed him; if he is thirsty, give him something to drink; for by so doing you will heap burning coals on his head.' Do not be overcome by evil, but overcome evil with*

good."

I don't know about you, but the last thing I want to do is give my enemy something to eat and drink. That heaping burning coals on his head thing sounds more like something I'd like to try. But let's look at these verses with our spiritual eyes for a minute so that we don't miss the beauty of what Paul's saying here.

Jesus called Himself the bread of life and living water (John 6:35; 7:37-38). When we love our enemies, when we choose to return their evil with good, we are in essence feeding them the same bread of life that gave life to our spirits and pouring upon them the living water that washed away our sins and made us children of God. We are showing them the love of God and the character of Christ. Doing this amplifies the depravity of their sin— making its presence in their lives burn hotly against their consciences like burning coals. And it may be the thing that nudges them to a place of repentance.

Whether an unintentional jab from a complete stranger or a life shaking blow from a close friend, make no mistake, whatever hurt you was an arrow skillfully shot by the powers of darkness. And the only way to defeat the dark is by shining the light of Christ.

Choose not to hold the sins of others against them. In letting go of your need for revenge, you give room for the only righteous Judge to mete out justice in His time and to call your enemy's heart to the very grace and forgiveness that changed you. Remember Matthew 5:9: "Blessed are the peacemakers, for they will be called children of God" (NIV).

Questions for Group and Personal Reflection:

1. What sins from your past tend to want to define you? How does it feel to know that God does not hold them against you anymore?

2. With what sin or temptation are you currently struggling? How can God's grace help you overcome it?

3. Whose forgiveness should you seek? Who needs your forgiveness? How does forgiving foil the enemy's plans?

4. Why do you think "peacemakers" are called "children of God" in Matthew 5:9?

Chapter 5

You Are Beautiful

"You are altogether beautiful, my love;

there is no flaw in you."

Song of Solomon 4:7

I want you to take a minute to close your eyes and think of all the images that come to mind when you think of the word "beautiful." Maybe you envision the sun setting on a cloudless horizon over the emerald waters of the ocean as it slowly begins to reflect the vibrant colors above. Maybe what you see is the flawless face of a supermodel as she sits perfectly poised on the cover of a magazine. Maybe you don't see anything at all but instead hear the unburdened melody of your favorite Mozart cantata.

If you were to ask a hundred different people to do that exercise, you'd probably get a hundred different answers regarding what is beautiful because, as they say, beauty is in the eye of the beholder. But, if I had to guess, I'd bet that one thing that did not cross your mind as you pondered beautiful things was you.

I say that because "beautiful" is not usually a word we women associate with ourselves. That's sad because we as God's daughters are much more beautiful than we tend to believe.

I suspect that a big part of why we women often think of ourselves as less than lovely boils down to our culture's narrow definition of what is physically attractive. The messages the world sends are deceitful and illusory. We women are encouraged to celebrate our uniqueness—

as long as it fits within certain, acceptable parameters. We're told to be our own kind of beautiful—as long as it measures up to some preset standards. But we all know that the trait that's most coveted and highly esteemed by our society is that of physical attractiveness—of the twenty-something, Hollywood starlet variety.

You can turn your television on any time of day or night and find countless commercials for makeup, skin care products, weight loss aids, and clothing. Every marketer promises us that if we will just use their product we will finally be able to achieve that higher standard of physical beauty for which we all long. But make no mistake, that "higher standard" is a large scale attack aimed directly at the hearts of women. For every commercial you see geared toward men, you will see a hundred more targeting female insecurities. Convincing us that we don't measure up.

God created humans with an ability to enjoy beauty and a desire to seek it out. Giving us the capacity to marvel over a snowy mountain range or to catch our breath at the sight of a field of wildflowers is one way of drawing us to Him, to the Creator of all things that are truly beautiful. But instead of seeking God when we see something that is lovely or instead of asking Him what it is that makes a woman beautiful, even we Christian women tend to bow to and even chase after the skewed image of feminine beauty that humanity has created.

As I thought on this, I realized that ever since Adam and Eve were in the garden, Satan has sought to twist our innate appreciation of visually beautiful things. In fact, he launched his first attack using the lure of beauty. Let's take a look at Genesis 3:6 to see what I mean: "When the woman saw that the fruit of the tree was good for food and pleasing to the eye, and also desirable for gaining wisdom, she took some and ate it. She also gave some to her husband, who was with her, and he ate it" (NIV).

Did you catch how Satan took Eve away from obedience to God and nudged her toward her own destruction? The fuller passage reveals that he used a carefully chosen question and denial of God's word that made her ignore what she knew was right in favor of taking a closer look at the fruit. And when she did that, she found it pleasing to the eye. Somehow its physical beauty helped to convince her that indulging in a taste of it couldn't be wrong. So she listened to Satan's promise that it would give her something that all the other trees God had given to them would not, equality with God. And tragically, instead of being satisfied with being in the presence of the beauty of God, Eve succumbed to the temptation to attempt to personify beauty in herself. It's a trap women fall for all the time.

Before we leave this Genesis passage, I want you to notice the order of events taking place in this exchange. Although Adam and Eve were there together, the serpent first drew the woman's attention to the fruit. I believe he did so because he was keenly aware of the power a woman's influence can have on the decision-making ability of men.

Think about it. Want to sell a car to a man? Drape a bikini-clad woman over the hood. Want to get a guy to eat your fast food chain's hamburgers? Make a commercial with a woman licking her pouty red lips while holding one of those burgers in her hand. Want millions of men to come see your movie? Make sure you've got a few scenes with scantily dressed women, who have nothing to do with the story line, dancing around in the background of your film's preview. Oh, and be sure to feature them on the playbill outside the movie theater as well. The outward attractiveness of a woman has been reduced to a marketing tool, a trophy, and a weapon. It is used to lure people with promises of pleasure, power, and success. We, however, are worth so much more than this.

God created males and females in His image (Genesis 1:26-27). And for a brief moment in time, we bore the flawless beauty of a sinless creation. But with Adam and Eve's initial rebellion came the shattering of that perfect world and the rise of depravity within the human heart. Now, instead of worshiping the God in whose image we were created, we worship idols created in our own image—things like age-defying bodies and sexual appeal. And if you and I want to fully live out the blessings of being God's daughters, it's time we stop bowing to those things and learn that we are inherently beautiful in His eyes.

Godly Beauty

To understand that God sees us as beautiful, we must first recognize that there is a stark contrast between worldly and godly beauty. Our culture puts so much emphasis on outward appearance and places little value on the beauty that lies within. Physical attractiveness, in fact, has become one of the key factors by which we as women measure our worth in this society. And since those standards are constantly changing with each new fashion line or trendy haircut's arrival, we can easily be left in constant pursuit. The Creator, by contrast, weighs beauty not by what's going on outside a person but by what's happening within her heart.

An example illustrating this point is found in First Samuel. Saul, the first king of Israel, was "a handsome young man. There was not a man among the people of Israel better looking than he. From his shoulders upward he was taller than any of the people" (1 Samuel 9:2). But in spite of his good looks and impressive height, Saul routinely made choices that displeased God. And God was ready to announce his replacement.

God told the prophet Samuel that he would find the new king He had chosen among the sons of Jesse the Bethlehemite (1 Samuel 16:1). The thing is, God didn't tell him which one of the sons to anoint as Israel's next human ruler. Samuel just had to trust that God would show him when he got there.

A glance at the boys led him to believe that the obvious choice would be Jesse's son, Eliab (1 Samuel 16:6). He was tall, strong, and good looking. Much like Saul, Eliab *looked* like he would be a good candidate for king. But listen to God's response to his prophet's thoughts in First Samuel 16:7: "Do not look on his appearance or on the height of his stature, because I have rejected him. For the LORD sees not as man sees: *man looks on the outward appearance, but the LORD looks on the heart*" (emphasis added).

In the end, Samuel had to ask Jesse whether he had any other sons because the Lord had not chosen any of those presented to him (1 Samuel 16:8-11). As it turned out, Jesse had been so sure that Samuel would choose one of his more impressive looking sons that instead of presenting him along with the others, he left David out in

119

the field tending sheep! Nevertheless, it was David who was God's choice of king. And importantly, it was David who Scripture heralds as being "a man after [God's] own heart" (1 Samuel 13:14).

God doesn't care about physical appearance. He cares about what's going on inside us.

Take a look at what Scripture says in 1 Peter 3:3-4: "Don't be concerned about the outward beauty of fancy hairstyles, expensive jewelry, or beautiful clothes. You should clothe yourselves instead with the beauty that comes from within, the unfading beauty of a gentle and quiet spirit, which is so precious to God" (NLT).

Why, since we know that God weighs beauty by what's happening on the inside and prefers that His girls clothe themselves with gentle spirits, do we Christian women still find ourselves working to earn the world's approval for our looks? And why is it that people in this world have a hard time distinguishing between those of God's kingdom and those of this world? I think the answer is that we tend to clothe ourselves in the garments of this world instead of putting on the beauty of God because it seems to be what everyone else is doing. Besides, most of us have either forgotten or were never taught what we are supposed to look like as Abba's daughters.

One verse in particular helps me to remember that being a woman after God's own heart is more important than having the most up-to-date wardrobe. Second Corinthians 3:18 says, "We all, with unveiled face, beholding the glory of the Lord, are being transformed into the same image from one degree of glory to another. For this comes from the Lord." This verse presents an underlying shift that is taking place inside everyone who has placed faith in Jesus Christ.

The key is in those words "being transformed." When we were reborn as daughters of the King, the enslaving sin that had shattered our ability to reflect the glory of our Creator was removed. Since those moments, we've been in the process of being transformed back into the image bearers we were created to be before sin messed things up. Thus, the inherent beauty within humanity that was lost in the garden is being restored within us! The Holy Spirit is cultivating in you and me, right now, the beauty of God's perfect creation. But we may not be able to see it until we start looking for it through the eyes of faith, not flesh.

As you allow God to transform your heart, you become ever more beautiful to Him and to anyone else who really gets to know you. God's kind of beauty transcends personal style. It's something that flows through our interactions and shines in our expressions. It radiates out from within us regardless of whether our clothes are preppy, edgy, conservative, or trendy. Godly beauty has nothing to do with the clothes you wear and remains present regardless of how the face that greets you in the mirror might change over time.

There is one woman in particular that comes to mind when I think of true beauty: Mrs. Mounts. She was my high school English teacher. She had big blond hair, long fingernails adorned with jewels and painted flowers, and she wore that bright blue eye shadow that epitomized late eighties makeup trends. Although she was indeed beautiful, an equally fitting description of her physical appearance might have been "glitzy." Nevertheless, she was absolutely beautiful to me because she so clearly loved every single kid that entered her class.

In fact, Mrs. Mounts fought for me at a time when I felt abandoned. She planted seeds of love in my heart when it seemed like my heart was nothing more than a barren wasteland. It was her way. She habitually saw the lost, consoled the hurting, and loved the broken. And she invested time in the ones who were on the right track too. No, it wasn't her flashy style that made kids run to her room as soon as the last bell sounded. It was the love that radiated from her. I will remember her forever as one of the most beautiful people I know.

The Beautiful Gate

As I was studying to write this chapter, the name of a certain gate that led into the Jerusalem temple came to mind. It's called the *Beautiful Gate*. There's not much said about this gate in the Bible. In fact, the only reference to it is in Acts 3:2, 10. Nevertheless, the name of this gate begged me to search out its significance.

You see, when the Jews were building the tabernacle and eventually the temple, the place where God's Spirit would dwell with His people, where they could worship and bring their offerings, deliberate and precise design was applied. Everything about the temple had divine significance. From the decorations on the building's walls, to its pillars and pedestals, to the lampstands and the altars within it, each item was a unique expression of God's character and His relationship with His people (see Exodus 35-40). So the addition of the Beautiful Gate, which was a feature of the restored temple standing in the days of Jesus, intrigued me.

Do you know what I found out through my research? Not much. In all my books, I found only a few paragraphs dedicated to this specific gate. Even so, I couldn't help but feel like God was saying there was more to the gate's existence, something deeper about it that He wanted me to see. So I prayed. And I reread the verses in

Acts. And I reread the bits of commentary I had found. And then, quite suddenly, it hit me.

The Beautiful Gate was named as such because it was the largest and most ornate gate in the temple complex. It was made out of "bronze that shone like gold."[17] But what was more amazing was not its size nor its appearance, but its placement in relation to the temple courts.

Four courtyards surrounded the temple. The inner court, which surrounded the temple itself, was the court of priests. Only Levitical priests who had fulfilled the laws of purification were allowed in this area. Next was the Court of Israel, which was accessible to all Jewish males. Outside that was the Court of Women. All Jewish people, male and female, were permitted there. These three courts sat on a platform above the outermost court and were accessible only to the covenant people of God.

The outermost court was called the Court of the Gentiles. It was not considered holy ground, so anyone was allowed into it. Importantly, between this court and the platform on which the other three courts were situated was a stone wall. On this wall were inscriptions written in both Greek and Latin stating that the penalty for non-Jews trying to go beyond that point was death. If you were not a child of God, you did not go past the outer court.

If you're a visual person like me sometimes a picture can help. This diagram, although not an exact scale, shows the basic layout so you can better visualize what I'm describing here.

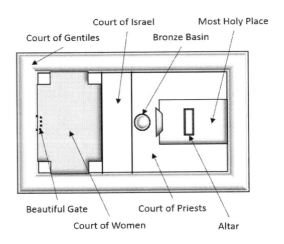

Here's where God's goodness and mercy started to unfold for me. Although since the destruction of the temple in AD 70, the exact knowledge of how the temple was laid out has been lost, it is believed that the Beautiful Gate was the passage leading from the Court of the Gentiles into the Court of Women. That means it was what separated those who were not part of the family of God from the presence of God. That big, beautiful, ornate gate was what the rest of the world could only peer through as they wondered what it must be like to be on the other side.

I don't believe there is any coincidence in the naming of this gate and its placement in the temple in which Jesus taught. True beauty draws us to the One who defines what beautiful really is. God invites us into the exquisite loveliness that He bestows. The shift that I was talking about earlier happens as we separate from the rest of the world and move into His presence. And when we move into His presence, as we begin to define our beauty by His standards, we become like the Beautiful Gate, inviting others into a relationship with our Heavenly Father.

Shifting Our Thinking

The knowledge that I don't have to strive after physical beauty anymore, that I only have to allow the Holy Spirit to transform me on the inside, is such a relief. It's a weight lifted off my burdened heart. But I admit that living in light of it has required some changes in my thinking, many of which didn't happen overnight.

So what are some practical ways you and I can begin to change the way we see beauty and begin to apply those heavenly standards to ourselves? What does this mean for all your make-up and clothes and all those shoes you have stored in your closet? Let me ease your mind by saying that I don't believe God wants us to ditch our beauty routines altogether and dress in potato sacks.

Instead, He wants us to stop trying to impress people with our appearance.

Whereas godly beauty comes from a longing for God's presence and a desire to bring glory to Him, it's worldly beauty that comes from a longing for other people's approval. Although our appearances may vary, there are a few key points we all need to understand and apply. The following lists highlight some of the differences:

Worldly Beauty	Godly Beauty
Enticing	Approachable
Alluring	Gentle
Sexy	Pure
Glamorous	Pleasing
Seductive	Refined
Intimidating	Welcoming
Subjective	Timeless
Powerful	Comforting
Evolving	Eternal
Outward	Inward

As if to highlight the difference between the two types of beauty, Paul wrote to his protégé Timothy that women "should adorn themselves in respectable apparel, with modesty and self-control, not with braided hair and gold or pearls or costly attire, but with what is proper for women who profess godliness—with good works" (1 Timothy 2:9-10). In our culture, much as in the culture prevalent when Paul wrote this, people place high value on one's ability to draw the gaze of others. There is a false sense of worth when we can cause the eyes of every man in a room to turn and lock on to us. However, the beauty we are meant to bear as daughters of our Heavenly Father isn't meant to catch someone's eye but to capture the heart. It's not meant to draw others to us but to point them to Christ.

When my husband Bill and I were first dating, I was young in my faith. Back then a lot of my self-esteem was tied up in how people saw me—especially in how men saw me. Capturing their interest gave me a distorted sense of worth and value. And if they didn't see me as beautiful, I reasoned, I must not be good enough.

Although in my younger years I did often dress in less than modest attire, I was dressing more appropriately by the time Bill and I met; nevertheless, my desire to be seen hadn't changed. My attitude toward other guys, which often revealed itself through little glances or facial expressions, gave the same impression that a skimpy skirt would.

There was a situation during the first years of our marriage, when Bill was still in the Marines and drilling at the reserve station in Atlanta, when I realized that something needed to change. At first I was flattered when he came home one day and told me that one of the guys was going to spray paint the words "Bennett's Hot Wife" on the wall of the hanger. But soon I felt embarrassed. I kind of liked the attention I was receiving, but at the same time I felt dirty and shamed by it. It wasn't long before God used that incident to work on me, and I realized that the only man I wanted to see me as sexy was my husband. Wanting the gaze of other men was wrong, and I needed God to change my heart.

In the coming months I considered the way I presented myself with fresh eyes. I gave careful thought to each interaction, aware that I wanted to be perceived differently than I had been in the past. I wanted to live in a way that honored my role as a daughter of the King and started giving deeper thought to what the Bible says on the subject. And it was at about that point that I started to embrace the idea that godly beauty is preferable to worldly beauty.

I'm delighted to report that having made the decision to present myself in such a way as to honor Jesus, I soon found that doing so became almost second nature. For instance, I determined to start intentionally smiling at people in public because I realized that even such a small gesture might be the only glimpse of kindness that some might receive in a day. After a while, I didn't think much of it. But last year a man approached me as I was walking into church. He wanted to tell me how much he enjoyed seeing my smile each Sunday. He told me to keep smiling like that because doing so was a blessing to others.

What a stark contrast this man's comment was with the "hot" comment made about me years before. As I thought about it, I realized that my overall appearance hadn't changed that much but my attitude had. And when I'd invited God to work on me and agreed to become more concerned with seeing the needs of others than with gaining attention for myself, the transformative work of the Holy Spirit had swept in and set my heart right.

There are days when I still struggle with wanting to be seen and desired and approved of because of my appearance. I am still very much a work in progress. But I can look at where I used to be and where I am now and see that God has brought me a long way. The more closely I walk with God, the more obvious it becomes that I am not the same person I used to be.

As daughters of our Heavenly Father, we are the temple where His Holy Spirit dwells (1 Corinthians 6:19). Doesn't it make perfect sense that our lives should serve as a beautiful gate inviting others to enter into a relationship with God?

Before we leave this chapter, I want us to take a moment to look more closely at the concept of being the modern temple of God because it is a much neglected, yet crucial, element of our identities as His children. And it reemphasizes our need to embody the beauty set by our Creator, not the world. Consider 2 Corinthians 6:16-18:

> *"What agreement is there between the temple of God and idols?* For we are the temple of the living God. *As God has said:*
>
> > *'I will live with them*
> > *and walk among them,*
> > *and I will be their God*
> > *and they will be my people.*
>
> Therefore
> > "Come out from them
> > and be separate,
> > *says the Lord,*
> > *Touch no unclean thing,*
> > *and I will receive you.*
>
> And
> > *I will be a Father to you,*
> > *and you will be my sons and daughters,*
> > *says the Lord Almighty.'"* (NIV; emphasis added)

This is a powerful and convicting portion of Scripture. Because we are the temple of the living God, we must have no part in the worship of idols. Therefore, the idol of physical beauty that is so pursued and sought by our culture needs to be identified as what it is. And should we find the desire to bow to it within our hearts, we must ask God to remove it and to replace it with His truth regarding beauty.

Romans 12:2 tells us not to follow the customs of this world but to allow God to transform us into new people by changing the way we think. When we focus on outward appearances, we are following the customs of the world. When we draw gazes toward ourselves, we are drawing them away from the glory of God. But when we choose to see true beauty the way our Father does, we position ourselves to encourage others to step out of the court of Gentiles and into His heavenly kingdom.

My sweet sister, true beauty has nothing to do with your dress size or your body type. It isn't about the color of your hair or your eyes. It's not the shape of your lips or the curve of your hips.

You are a daughter of God! Your curly, wild hair is beautiful. Your masses of sun-kissed freckles are beautiful. Your slender hips and lanky legs are beautiful. Your six foot and two inch high frame is beautiful. Your crooked nose, your scars, your so-called imperfections, they are beautiful! Because they belong to you.

Yes, because of Jesus you are seen as flawless in the eyes of your Creator. Therefore, let your life and your appearance be representative of the redemption that was purchased for you on the cross. Outwardly express the inner person who is being transformed into the image of Christ.

You, my dear sister, are beautiful!

Questions for Group and Personal Reflection:

1. Why is a pursuit of worldly beauty so dangerous for us as God's daughters?

2. In what ways do you personally need to realign your perception of beauty to the way God wants you to see it?

3. What about yourself have you called ugly that God wants you to see as beautiful?

4. How can you make your life like a beautiful gate inviting others into the presence of God?

Chapter 6

You Are Enough

"I can do all things through [Christ]

who strengthens me."

Philippians 4:13

As I've talked with women over the years, I have discovered that a common thread weaves its way through most of our lives. That thread is a feeling of inadequacy. For some the feeling is focused internally in that we doubt our own value or usefulness. We believe that we are somehow insufficient for the task at hand, whatever it may be. For others this sense stems from external things. We believe that what we have is not enough. Deep down we're sure that we need more money, a better job, smarter kids, or a larger home to have or be enough. A single root feeds both tendencies: Satan challenges our belief in God's sufficiency for our lives.

All throughout Scripture we find stories of people who felt less than qualified for their callings or believed that what they had in front of them was insufficient to meet their needs. Moses believed his speech impediment would hinder his ability to speak to Pharaoh as instructed (Exodus 3:11—4:12). Thirty-eight of the forty Israelite spies sent to scout out the land God had promised to give them brought back a false report because they were afraid of the natives who were living there, as if they were an insurmountable obstacle (Numbers 13). Even the disciples who had been living with Jesus doubted His ability to feed a large crowd—even though He had already provided for an even larger crowd just a short time before (Matthew 14:13-21; 15:32-38). In every circumstance of what seemed a glaring inadequacy from man's perspective,

God proved His provision, power, and providence in the face of human weakness.

Maybe you're frustrated with being a stay-at-home mom, and you miss the career you worked so hard to establish before you had kids. Maybe your husband isn't as romantic as your best friend's husband, and you feel neglected in your marriage. Maybe you've been struggling with a chronic illness, and you wonder why you have to suffer. Perhaps you are single and longing for a family of your own. It could be that you are in your forties, finding yourself back in school and practically starting life all over again. Maybe you feel like your job isn't important enough or your house isn't nice enough or your family isn't gifted enough. Something in your life just doesn't feel like it's enough. And even if you can rationalize that feeling away by telling yourself that whatever it is isn't so bad or perhaps isn't as limiting as you fear, where you are is just not where you expected to be when you mapped out your life plan. And you can't help but feel discouraged about it.

I think all of us become discontent with our lives at one point or another. But although these feelings are nothing out of the ordinary, they are contrary to the way God wants us to view our lives as His daughters. So we need to give this subject some attention.

Frankly, I have battled feelings of inadequacy in lots of things throughout my life. Am I a good enough mother? Am I really the wife my husband needs me to be? Do I help others enough? Am I strong enough to handle the weight of life's demands? And most recently, am I the right person to be writing this book? But over and over God has responded to my concerns with this Scripture: "My grace is sufficient for you, for my power is made perfect in weakness." So, like the apostle Paul to whom the Lord first spoke these words, "I will boast all the more gladly in my weaknesses, so the power of Christ may rest upon me" (2 Corinthians 12:9).

There is so much wisdom and truth packed into this one verse! It has become what I call my "life verse." So let's get out our magnifiers again and look a little more closely at all the freeing details hidden here.

But God

In 2 Corinthians 12:8 Paul pleaded with the Lord to remove a certain difficulty from his life. Rather than doing what was requested, however, God responded to him with a promise of God's own sufficiency. What I don't want you to miss in the lead up to our discussion of that promise are the five words introducing God's reply to Paul: "But he said to me" (2 Corinthians 12:9). I love that! Paul admitted an inadequacy. Then God stepped in and basically said, "Let me tell you what I have to say about that."

As I thought on this, it reminded me that God always has the last word on our circumstances because He knows, from beginning to end, all that we're going to need. I realized that the phrase "but God" is a game changer for those willing to admit their need for His help. There is so much power and promise in those two little words. No matter what we are facing or feel that we are lacking, those words remind us that God is enough, that He is sovereign, and that if God is for us, no one can really stand against us (Romans 8:31). While the phrase is not stated explicitly in the text of the following references, here are just a few "but God" promises I've found in His Word:

I feel inadequate ... but God is enough. (2 Cor. 9:8)
I feel afraid ... but God is in control. (Isa. 43:2)
I feel weak ... but God is strong. (1 Cor. 10:13)
I feel unworthy ... but God is merciful. (Heb. 4:16)
I feel unsure ... but God is my confidence. (Prov. 3:26)
I feel useless ... but God is my purpose. (Col. 3:23-24)
I feel lacking ... but God is my portion. (Lam. 3:24)

There is a "but God ..." for every circumstance we will ever face.

Before we dive more deeply into other takeaways we can glean from 2 Corinthians 12:9, I want to speak for a moment about the personal sense of insufficiency, the "thorn" in Paul's side, that he had repeatedly pleaded with God to remove (2 Corinthians 12:7). No one knows exactly what this thorn was; it could have been a physical ailment or defect or an internal struggle or temptation that he had been unable to overcome completely. Whatever the case, God chose not to remove the thorn but left it in Paul's life as a reminder that His grace alone was sufficient in helping Paul meet life's challenges. It reminded Paul that on his own, he really wasn't enough— but God was.

Prior to him coming to faith in Jesus as Messiah Paul was a proud and zealous Pharisee responsible for much of the persecution of the early church and even gave approval of the first martyrdom of a Christ-follower, Stephen (Acts 7:57—8:1). Paul (also known as Saul) was educated, respected, and steadily climbing the ranks of the religious hierarchy when Jesus turned his world upside down. It seems that prior to that encounter his pride in the law and in his own knowledge and position fueled his anger toward those who proclaimed the message of Christ. But once the man became a follower of Jesus himself and was growing in wisdom and authority as an apostle, he surely found that old habits can be difficult to shake. It would have been very easy for pride to creep its way into a place of dominance in his heart.

So Paul wisely took his "not enough," whatever that thorn he'd been dealt was, and gave it to God in prayer. This lack, or need, became his pipeline to his Father's abundance. In time Paul's struggle became his praise because he knew the thorn would keep him dependent on His relationship with God. Rather than trying to have it all together, Paul learned to embrace his thorn as a way to show other people like me, who don't have it all together either, their need to rely on God.

Sufficient Grace

I wish I could express in a few words how truly wonderful it is that God told Paul, "My grace is sufficient for you" (2 Corinthians 12:9). "Grace" is defined as the divine favor and benefit we receive as God's children. It is a gift reserved strictly for His sons and daughters. His grace is seen in its influence on our hearts and its reflection in our lives. It is what enables us to persevere in our Christian walk (Acts 20:32). And it's not something given because we deserve it. It is unmerited kindness given by a loving Father.

What makes God's grace so amazing is that it is entirely sufficient for whatever we are facing. The Greek word for sufficient in this verse means to assist or satisfy, and to avail. God's grace will fortify us in our weakness, satisfy our longings, and be our ever-present help in times

141

of trouble (Psalm 46:1). So, whether God chooses to take away our personal thorns or not, we can be as sure as Paul was that His grace is sufficient for us too.

Perfect Power

I love that God assured Paul, "My power is made perfect in weakness" (2 Corinthians 12:9). This is really special because it tells us that God isn't expecting us to handle all of life's hurdles ourselves, pushing through on will power, cunning, and physical strength. Rather, He wants us to know that it is in our weakest moments that we give Him the best chance to show off how strong and helpful He really is.

The idea of human weaknesses being a conduit through which God can work seems a little counterintuitive as first. But let me explain. I was brought up to be independent and self-sufficient. But there was a time in my life when I'd dug myself into such a deep pit that there was no way I could have climbed out of it on my own. And there was no way my own strength could have carried me through the months that followed. Yet interestingly, it was in that state of helplessness that I first experienced God's perfect power at work in my life. And as a result of that, I have learned to draw on God's strength rather than my own.

Paul too learned to draw on God's perfect power throughout his life and ministry. By the time he wrote this second letter to the church at Corinth, Paul had been through a lot: shipwrecks, severe beatings, imprisonment, persecution. And if anyone had just cause to throw in the towel, he did. Nevertheless, Paul didn't grumble or complain. He leaned on the Lord for help, even writing about it in his letter to the Philippian church (which he wrote while he was in prison). He said, "I know how to be brought low, and I know how to abound. In any and every circumstance, I have learned the secret of facing plenty and hunger, abundance and need. I can do all things through him who strengthens me" (Philippians 4:12-13). Indeed, our strength lies not in our own ability or resources but in God's power.

The word translated "perfect" in 2 Corinthians 12:9 carries with it the idea of consecration. To consecrate something means to make or declare it holy or to set it apart for a divine purpose. When God's perfect power is welcome in our lives, then, He is able to fulfill in us the divine purpose for which we were created. God's holiness overtakes our weaknesses so that He can accomplish His sovereign will in and through us.

I love the way we see this principle illustrated in the lives of the first disciples. Jesus chose to walk out His time on earth not with religious scholars or men with great political influence. Instead, He chose to live alongside ordinary men. One of them in fact, Matthew, had been a tax collector. That was considered nearly the equivalent of a traitor to the Jewish community! But God empowered each of these men to meet the challenges before them— not in their own strength but with His mighty power flowing through them.

Just look at what this passage from Acts says about two of them: "Now when [the religious leaders] saw the boldness of Peter and John, and perceived that they were uneducated, common men, they were astonished. And they recognized that they had been with Jesus" (Acts 4:13).

Isn't that a powerful testimony of God's power at work in the lives of His people? It is certainly what I want people to say when they look at you and me. May people observe the fruit of our lives, at what we can do as the Lord moves through us, and say, "Wow! She *must* have been with Jesus!"

Our innate weakness points to God's strength. The purpose of any lack we perceive in our lives should point to God's supply. And when we notice a sense of discontent with the world in those with whom we interact, we must recognize that therein is an opportunity to point to the ultimate satisfaction found only in a relationship with our Heavenly Father.

I pray that whatever your weakness or your struggles, your short-comings or your imperfections, you'll give them to God and ask Him to work through those things for His glory. Carry all such concerns to the cross and lay them down at His feet. Let Him fill you with a sense of His all-sufficient grace and cover your lack with His perfect power.

A Purpose Beyond What We Can See

I don't want to close this discussion of God's power at work within His people without bringing to light a certain story that always blesses me. It's a wonderful reminder that on the days when we feel insignificant, when we wonder whether anything good can come out of our mundane lives or out of what seems to us to be not enough, that our God really is at work through us. And often on a scale we can't imagine! His plans for His sons and daughters, in fact, are directly linked to His bigger plan for humankind. One small act of kindness can change the course of a life.

Hilde Back is a name that's unfamiliar to most. Much of her life was not what many would consider extraordinary; nevertheless, the Lord clearly worked through her.

As a preschool teacher in Sweden, Hilde did not have tremendous financial means. Yet even with her limited ability, Hilde made the decision to do what she could. She decided to sponsor the education of a child living in Kenya, having learned that many poor children there have little hope of escaping their extreme poverty without schooling—something which most of them cannot afford. Thanks to Hilde's generosity, Chris Mburu was able to avoid an impoverished fate.

Not only was Chris able to complete his secondary education, but he went on to study at the University of Nairobi and then continued on to Harvard Law School. In time Chris became a Human Rights Advocate for the United Nations and eventually started his own charity (The Hilde Back Education Fund) that pays tuition for other children living in Kenya. Hilde's one small act of kindness has thus impacted the lives of hundreds of children—a blessing which in turn impacts their families and villages as well.

What's even more amazing about this story is that it was another act of kindness from a stranger that saved Hilde's own life. Hilde was a Jewish girl living in Germany during the Nazi reign. When both of her parents were killed, a stranger was able to help Hilde escape to Sweden, which not only saved her life but enabled her to receive the education she'd been denied as a Jew living in Germany. It was, in fact, her personal knowledge of the necessity and privilege of an education that became the catalyst behind her decision to sponsor the education of one, seemingly insignificant, boy.[18]

When we allow ourselves to focus on a lie that we aren't enough—whether it's the lie that we aren't good enough, rich enough, important enough, or appreciated enough—we may miss out on God-given opportunities to be a blessing. Feeding our insecurities, in fact, is one method Satan uses to turn our eyes away from the One who is enough. We must remember that we can only fulfill the purposes intended for our lives when we rely on God's sufficient grace and perfect power to be enough even if we aren't—and thus trust His sovereign plan.

The Body of Christ

As followers of Christ and daughters of our Heavenly Father, we are to function as members of one body at work for the good of others. When we neglect to appreciate the specific roles God has assigned to us, the whole body starts to suffer.

> *"Indeed, the body is not one part but many. If the foot should say, 'Because I'm not a hand, I don't belong to the body,' it is not for that reason any less a part of the body. And if the ear should say, 'Because I'm not an eye, I don't belong to the body,' it is not for that reason any less a part of the body.*

147

If the whole body were an eye, where would the hearing be? If the whole body were an ear, where would the sense of smell be? But as it is, God has arranged each one of the parts in the body just as he wanted. And if they were all the same part, where would the body be? As it is, there are many parts, but one body." (1 Corinthians 12:14-20, CSB)

When I read this in light of this chapter's theme, I'm reminded of two parts of our physical bodies: the appendix and the mesentery. For a long time scientists were unable to figure out what the purpose of the appendix was. In fact, as far as they were concerned, it served no purpose. Today, however, while there are conflicting theories about what it does precisely, most feel confident that it is not without a role. In 2016 scientists officially classified an entirely new organ called the mesentery, which is a small fold of tissues that attaches the intestine to the wall of the abdomen. The mesentery is something that has always been there but because of its seemingly insignificant appearance it had long been overlooked when anatomy was discussed. Today, however, the medical community realizes it plays a vital role in helping supply our blood vessels, lymphatic systems, and nerves with the nutrients they need.

There may be times when we feel a bit like an appendix or a mesentery, as if the purpose for our lives is either a big mystery or perhaps our value has been overlooked entirely. But make no mistake: God formed you with a specific purpose in mind. First and foremost, He wanted to have a relationship with you through the faith you'd place in His rescue plan, Jesus. Second, He wanted to radiate His glory to the world through you— and He may well intend to accomplish that in ways you have yet to envision.

What I hope you'll remember the next time a sense of inadequacy comes calling, sister, is that you were never meant to be enough on your own. You were created to be a conduit connected to the One who is enough, who wants to radiate His sufficiency in and through you. So in all that you do, whether you're raising kids, running a company, cleaning bathrooms, storming gates, or simply facing one day at a time, don't forget that your purpose is to glorify God. In doing that, you'll find that you really are enough.

God is able to do with our weaknesses more than you or I could ask, think, or imagine (Ephesians 3:20). So let the knowledge that God is enough for whatever season you are in stir you on to confident obedience in the things you are facing today—in the scary, the difficult, the uncertain, and the mundane—so that in doing so you will shine your light to the world and glorify your Father in heaven (Matthew 5:16).

Questions for Group and Personal Reflection:

1. In what area of your life do you most struggle with feelings of inadequacy?

2. How might calling to mind 2 Corinthians 12:9 encourage you the next time you feel inadequate?

3. How does the knowledge that God can work through our lives in ways we can't immediately see—as in Hilde's case—encourage you?

4. Are you willing to let God use your sense of inadequacy to draw you into a deeper dependence on Him? Explain.

Chapter 7

You Are Mine

"See what kind of love the Father has given to us,

that we should be called children of God;

and so we are."

1 John 3:1

The reality of our identity as heirs of our Heavenly Father is so rich and vast that one book could never cover it completely. Nevertheless, I hope that as we come to the final chapter of this journey together, you have arrived at a deeper, more satisfying, and more solidly anchored understanding of the One who created you as well as who you are because you are His.

There is something sacred about our position as Abba's daughters. We belong to Him—not as slaves but as family members. God hasn't bound us with shackles; He's drawn us close to His heart and given us His name. He has paid our sin debt and given us an inheritance among His children. Remarkably, God Himself answers all our fears, doubts, insecurities, questions, longings, and hesitations with one simple statement: "You are mine." And it is in these three words that we find everything we'll ever need.

Psalm 103:2 tells us to "bless the LORD ... and forget not all his benefits," so let's take a minute to recap the truths we've learned so far. A quick reminder will position our hearts to embrace why living out these truths is so important.

1. You are chosen. You are not only wanted but cherished and highly regarded by an infinite, almighty, and all-knowing God. Before the foundation of the world, God wanted *you* to be His child (Ephesians 1:4). The One who created the galaxies desires a personal relationship with you.

You weren't chosen, though, because you were worthy of being picked. It wasn't because of anything you did or did not do. You are worthy only because God wanted to make it so. He picked you to reflect His image, to bear His name, and to be with Him for eternity. And all you had to do was place your trust in Jesus.

2. You are loved. God's love for you is not a fickle "love" dependent on your performance. It is not something that shifts or changes over time. His love is eternal, faithful, and constant. It is not the wax-fruit-type imposter the world tries to pass off as love. Rather, God's love is the very core of His divine DNA (1 John 4:8). It's not just something that He acts out, but something that He embodies.

This love is the very thing that has sustained His faithfulness to all generations (Psalm 100:5). It is what motivated His decision to sacrifice His own Son in our place (John 3:16). It is the source from which His provision for His children flows (Psalm 111:5). God's love, poured out in you through His Holy Spirit, is what enables you to live a life that honors Him and serves others (1 John 4:7; 5:2).

3. You are reborn. The moment you put your faith in the saving work of Jesus Christ you became a new creation. Your old nature passed away, and you were given new life as a child of God (Romans 6:6). It is this rebirth that solidifies a believer's place in God's family and brings about the fulfillment of all the promises God has for His children.

New birth, though, is just the beginning of the new life you received through Christ. It washed off your old, sinful nature (Titus 3:5), and you also received a new heart and a new spirit. On top of that, you received the Holy Spirit—who came to dwell within you—to help you live out your new life in full obedience to God's will (1 Corinthians 3:16; Ezekiel 36:25-27). When nurtured, the seed planted in a heart at the moment of rebirth will grow until its bearer becomes a tree of righteousness bearing good fruit according to the Father's good will.

4. You are forgiven. The sins that once separated you from God have been washed away. Nothing from your past will be counted against you because the blood of Christ shed on the cross has paid the price for your freedom. You have been given the free gift of eternal life that not only atones for your past but also empowers your present and future ability to live for righteousness.

Our Heavenly Father knows the devastating pull sin has on us, so He saturated His forgiveness with the grace we need to overcome the temptations of this world and walk in liberty. His desire is that we as His children not fall back under the yoke of slavery to sin but live in the freedom we have been given.

The Bible teaches us that there is no condemnation for those in Christ (Romans 8:1). That means that while we must take care never to take a light attitude toward sin in our lives, we don't have to be afraid of messing up or making mistakes. God's not going to write you off or disown you! You are His beloved daughter now and forever. And because of that, He wants you to model forgiveness and grace by seeking and extending them in your interactions with others.

5. You are beautiful. As God's daughter, you no longer have to chase after unattainable standards. You don't have to depend on your outer appearance for gaining approval. You do not have to pursue beautiful things; rather, you are to pursue the One who makes things beautiful. Remember, true beauty is not achieved by conforming to the world's standards but by being transformed into the image of our Father. It is an outer reflection of your renewed inner person that is expressed through things like humility, kindness, modesty, and gentleness.

Never forget that true beauty isn't meant to make people see you; instead, it's intended to help people see beyond you to your Heavenly Father. It is an evidence of the new life made available to those who are in Christ. Exposure to true, godly, heavenly beauty stirs conviction and offers hope. It has nothing to do with personal style; it's all about having a personal relationship with God.

6. *You are enough.* Being enough isn't about personal ability or strength. It's not about being independent or self-sufficient. It is about drawing on the grace that is perfected in your weakness. It is having the courage to trust that God is enough even though you aren't. It's trusting that God is sovereign in all circumstances and has the power to make a way even when you can't see how a way could be made.

God's grace is what sustains us and equips us in our obedience to His calling on our lives. Personal weaknesses, then, aren't disqualifications; instead, they are intended to prompt us to a necessary, humble disposition that keeps us dependent on God and propels us into a deeper relationship with our Source of strength.

Bringing These Truths Home

Perhaps as this book draws to a close, you find yourself feeling a little uncertain about whether one or more of the points about a believer's identity in Christ really belong to you. Maybe you feel like the exception. Let me remind you of the source from which the truths in this volume came. Every point has been mined from the Word of God like the precious jewel that it is. And each supports the underlying truth of Romans 3:22, which states, "We are made right with God by placing our faith in Jesus Christ. And this is true for *everyone who believes, no matter who [they] are*" (NLT; emphasis added).

It doesn't matter where you've been or what you've done. All you have to do is believe that you are now God's daughter simply because you accepted the grace He extended you through Christ. There may be times when you'll struggle with your belief, but please remember that a believer's struggle does not negate God's steadfastness. God is not going to change His mind about you because just as sure as there's nothing from your past that could prevent His ability to redeem you as His, there is nothing in your future that could separate you from His love (Romans 8:38). God even "bound himself with an oath" so that we who have received His promise through Christ Jesus could be completely confident "that He would never change His mind" (Hebrews 6:17).

First Peter 1:3-5 helps me to lay aside any doubt about my position in God's family. It reminds me that the benefits promised to me in this life are only a hint of the wonders to come:

"Blessed be the God and Father of our Lord Jesus Christ! According to his great mercy, he has caused us to be born again to a living hope through the resurrection of Jesus Christ from the dead, to an inheritance that is imperishable, undefiled, and unfading, kept in heaven for [us], who by God's power are being guarded through faith for a salvation ready to be revealed in the last time."

That passage is talking about our eternal future with Jesus. When that time comes, our Father "will wipe away every tear from [our] eyes, and death shall be no more, neither shall there be mourning, nor crying, nor pain anymore, for the former things [will] have passed away" (Revelation 21:4).

This is what we are journeying toward on our paths through this life and why we, as Abba's daughters, are not to concern ourselves with the pursuits of this world. We need to keep our eyes on the prize, so to speak, so that we don't get distracted. This is what Paul was speaking of when he said, "I press on toward the goal for the prize of the upward call of God in Christ Jesus" (Philippians 3:14).

When Jesus returns to set up His sinless, perfectly wonderful kingdom at time's end, the nations will be gathered before Him. At that point, Scripture says, He will permanently separate the sheep (His followers of all times and places) from the goats (non-believers) like the Good Shepherd that He is. It is then that we will receive the full inheritance promised to us by our Heavenly Father. To us Jesus will say, "Come, you who are blessed by my Father, inherit the kingdom prepared for you from the foundation of the world" (Matthew 25:31-34).

Living on Mission

Few in my biological family live close together. We're all a seven hours drive or longer away from each other. So, when we can get everyone together in the same place at the same time, it's pretty close to a miracle. And I enjoy those events so much that when it's time to say goodbye, I can draw things out like nobody's business. I don't like knowing that it might be a really long time until I see people I love again.

I bring this up because both heaven, the destination promised to believers who pass away, and hell, the future address of those who refuse to accept Christ, are realities. Every person you know will inevitably end up either in God's presence or detached from Him for eternity (Revelation 20:15). And as sure as I'm excited about my own eternal future, this truth makes me really sad because I have family members and friends I love dearly that have not placed their faith in Jesus. And as much as it hurts to know it might be a while before I see them again I don't even want to think that I might never see them again.

Here is where the sacredness of our belonging to God becomes glaringly significant for the lives of those we know. When God says, "You are Mine," that implies that we are to be set apart for Him. That we have work to do on His behalf. Because you and I belong to God, we are a kingdom of priests, part of a holy nation tasked with sharing the truth of the gospel (1 Peter 2:9; Mark 16:15-16). We are a people God formed for Himself so that we might declare His praise to the world (Isaiah 43:21). Matthew 5:16 tells us to "let [our] light shine before others, so that they may see [our] good works and give glory to [our] Father who is in heaven."

Just before this verse in Matthew, Jesus reminded us that people don't hide lamps under a basket. We put them on a table or someplace where their light can radiate throughout our homes (Matthew 5:15). He said that because we as God's daughters (or sons) serve as God's light in this sin-darkened world. We are here to point others to the Father as often as we can so that they too can come to share in the future hope and new life that we enjoy.

Sadly, though, many of God's children are neglecting their duties. And before closing, I want to point out that we must remain on mission. We can't just be silent about Jesus. We can't live selfishly. We must not fall into a pattern of just aimlessly living as if today is all there is. When we look more like the world than we do our Heavenly Father, we are withholding from others the truth of God's goodness and hope for all who believe (1 Timothy 4:10). We are robbing them of the opportunity to see God's glory through us. And allowing that to happen is especially tragic when measured against the lengths God went to so that we could be His.

If you haven't already experienced the temptation to put your faith on the back burner or if you do find yourself neglecting to live out your role as God's daughter on occasion, let me tell you a little bit about the situation in which Daniel (of lion's den fame) found himself. It sheds light on one of Satan's most effective tactics against us.

Daniel, along other Jewish men, was exiled from his homeland and forced to live in Babylon. It was a world empire that reigned for several hundred years but reached its height around 600 BC. The nation's kings loved to fight and conquer and expand their territory. And through all their conquering, they learned some successful ways to subdue the inhabitants of the territories they captured.

163

Unlike other rulers who enslaved their captives, Babylon sought to assimilate them. And assimilation is just what the Babylonian king had in mind for Daniel and his friends:

> *"The king commanded Ashpenaz, his chief eunuch, to bring some of the people of Israel, both of the royal family and of the nobility, youths without blemish, of good appearance and skillful in all wisdom, endowed with knowledge, understanding learning, and competent to stand in the king's palace, and to teach them the literature and language of the Chaldeans [that is, of the Babylonians]. The king assigned them a daily portion of the food that the king ate, and of the wine that he drank. They were to be educated for three years, and at the end of that time they were to stand before the king."* (Daniel 1:3-5)

Daniel's homeland had been decimated by the time he was taken to this pagan ruler's palace. Solomon's temple was destroyed, and Jerusalem's walls were leveled. Babylon, by contrast, was a rich and lavish place with beautiful architecture, an advanced education system, a booming economy, powerful rulers, and all the ingredients needed for a pleasure-filled life. So how tempting would it be for this newly conquered captive, Daniel, to take the opportunity to join people in the extravagance offered? Yet, as the book bearing his name reveals, this young man and his friends refused to be stripped of their culture. They didn't compromise their faith to indulge in worldly pleasure. They were forced to live among the Babylonians, yet they remained distinct and committed to honoring God and His preferences. It seems these Hebrew boys realized that there was no better way to subdue God's people than to make them fall in love with a different way of life; thus, they wisely refused to fall for Babylon's ploy.

Did you know that Satan wants us to fall in love with the things of this world so we will be distracted from the things of God? He wants us to pursue worldly pleasures rather than heavenly treasures (Matthew 6:20). But we must remember that our lives speak to those on the outside looking in. We believers are ambassadors of heaven, and the way we live shapes others' view of God. So, the same way we had to strip away the lies we'd believed about our Heavenly Father so that we could come to know the reality of who He is, we also need to strip away from ourselves anything that falsely represents who He is to the world around us. As 1 John 3:10 says, "By this it is evident who are the children of God, and who are the children of the devil: whoever does not practice righteousness is not of God, nor is the one who does not love his brother."

We are to be holy just as our Father is holy (1 Peter 1:15-16). We are to be set apart for the Gospel of God (Romans 1:1). We are to remain distinct from the culture around us just as Daniel did in Babylon. It's a tall order, I know. But as we discussed in the last chapter, God's strength is perfected in our weakness. Because of the power of the Holy Spirit in us we can live lives that indeed speak to the fact that we are His.

I so appreciate what Ephesians 2:12-13 and 19 say:

> *"Remember that you were ... separated from Christ, alienated from the commonwealth of Israel and strangers to the covenants of promise, having no hope and without God in the world. But now in Christ Jesus you who once were far off have been brought near by the blood of Christ. ... So then you are no longer strangers and aliens, but you are fellow citizens with the saints and members of the household of God."*

You have been "brought near by the blood of Christ." You are a saint, God's treasured possession. You are chosen, hand-picked by a holy God, created to bear His image. You are fully known and fully loved with no strings attached. You have been reborn into God's family, redeemed at a price only He could pay. You have been forgiven, exonerated from all guilt or shame from your past. And you are empowered by God's own Spirit to live free from the bondage of sin. You are beautiful, radiant with the glory of God's transforming grace. Whoever you are, whatever you have or lack, you are enough because God's sufficient grace will strengthen and assist you.

Dear sister, let us seek to glorify God, our Father. He has redeemed us from death, brought us into new life, and He has good works for us to do (2 Timothy 2:21). Let's take advantage of every opportunity to live in light of our new identity in Christ and to help others know of the freedom and purpose offered to anyone who asks to be adopted into His family through placing faith in Jesus. Because, after all, we are Abba's daughters.

Questions for Group and Personal Reflection:

1. Which characteristic associated with being God's daughter has been the most impactful for you as you've read this book? Why?

2. How does it feel to know that God says of you, "You are mine"?

3. What are some practical ways that you can avoid conforming to the world's ways instead of God's?

4. With whom will you share the good news of Jesus this week?

You Are Mine

About The Author

"Having a lifelong love for writing and coming from a long line of teachers, it was no surprise when God combined Jennifer's personal passion with her genetic inclination when He called her to follow Him. Teaching in women's and children's ministry, developing Bible study curriculum, and authoring her book, *Abba's Daughter,* have all been driven by her desire for people to truly understand the heart of their Heavenly Father - something that has greatly impacted her own life as she has learned to trust in His love for her. Jennifer loves to dig deep into the depths of scripture and the heart of God, living out what the Lord shows her and sharing it with others every chance she gets.

Jennifer is a wife, mother, and grandmother, living in southern Alabama with her family. Along with her love for writing, teaching, and family time, Jennifer's passion is pottery, which she considers both her creative outlet and her therapy."

To contact Jennifer, feel free to e-mail her at: *ascarletcord221@gmail.com* or you can visit her blog: *http://www.ascarletcord.wordpress.com*. You can also follow her on Facebook: *@ascarletcord*.

Notes

1. Eric J. Alexander, *Our Great God and Saviour* (East Peoria, IL: Versa Press, 2010), 4.
2. For a wonderful visual aid on this topic, see Francis Chan, "The Awe Factor of God" *youtube.com: https://www.youtube.com/watch?v=3Ya12I036lg.* (November 8, 2010).
3. Elizabeth Howell, "How Many Stars are in the Universe?" *Space.com*: *https://www.space.com/26078-how-many-stars-are-there.html.* (May 17, 2017).
4. Eric Metaxas, "Science Increasingly Makes the Case for God," *Wall Street Journal*: *https://www.wsj.com/articles/eric-metaxas-science-increasingly-makes-the-case-for-god-1419544568* (December 25, 2014).
5. Chris Baraniuk, "It Took Centuries, But We Now Know the Size of the Universe," *BBCEarth.com: http://www.bbc.com/earth/story/20160610-it-took-centuries-but-we-now-know-the-size-of-the-universe* (June 13, 2016).

6. James Strong, *Strong's Comprehensive Concordance of the Bible* (Iowa Falls, IA: World Bible Publishers, 1986) s. v. "love."

7. Timothy R. Jennings, *The God Shaped Brain: How Changing Your View of God Transforms Your Life* (Downer's Grove, IL: Intervarsity Press, 2013), 22.

8. W. E. Vine, *Expository Dictionary of New Testament Words*, vol. 3 (Nashville, TN: Thomas Nelson, 1996): 21.

9. Ibid.

10. Marcus Dods, *Expositor's Bible Commentary: 1 Corinthians*, ed. Rev. W. Robertson Nicoll, excerpt taken from commentary on 1 Corinthians 13:4-13 as found on the e-Sword Bible study software program. Public domain.

11. Strong, s. v. "beareth."

12. "Fruit Trees: Years to Fruit," StarkBros: *https://www.starkbros.com/growing-guide/article/how-many-years.*

13. Alistair Begg, *Made For His Pleasure: Ten Benchmarks of a Vital Faith* (Chicago, IL: Moody Publishers, 1996), 16.

14. J. D. Douglas and Merrill C. Tenny, *Zondervan Illustrated Bible Dictionary* ed. Moisés Silva. (Grand Rapids, MI: Zondervan, 2011), 548.

15. Eric Metaxas, *Bonhoeffer: Pastor, Martyr, Prophet, Spy* (Nashville, TN, Thomas Nelson Publishers, 2010), 486

16. Neil T. Anderson, *The Bondage Breaker Small Group Bible Study: Student Guide* (Ventura, CA: Gospel Light, 2004), 47.

17. J. D. Douglas and Merrill C. Tenny, *Zondervan Illustrated Bible Dictionary* ed. Moisés Silva. (Grand Rapids, MI: Zondervan, 2011), 174.

18. For more on Hilde Beck's story, see Brad Aronson, "Hilde Back—The Amazing Story of How One Woman's Small Acts of Kindness Changed Over 350 Lives" *https://www.bradaronson.com/small-acts-of-kindness/.*

Made in the USA
Columbia, SC
18 July 2021